HOMO SAPIENS PART VII

SEVENTEEN POEMS TO EXPLORE THE CONDITIONS OF HUMANITY

MAWPHNIANG NAPOLEON

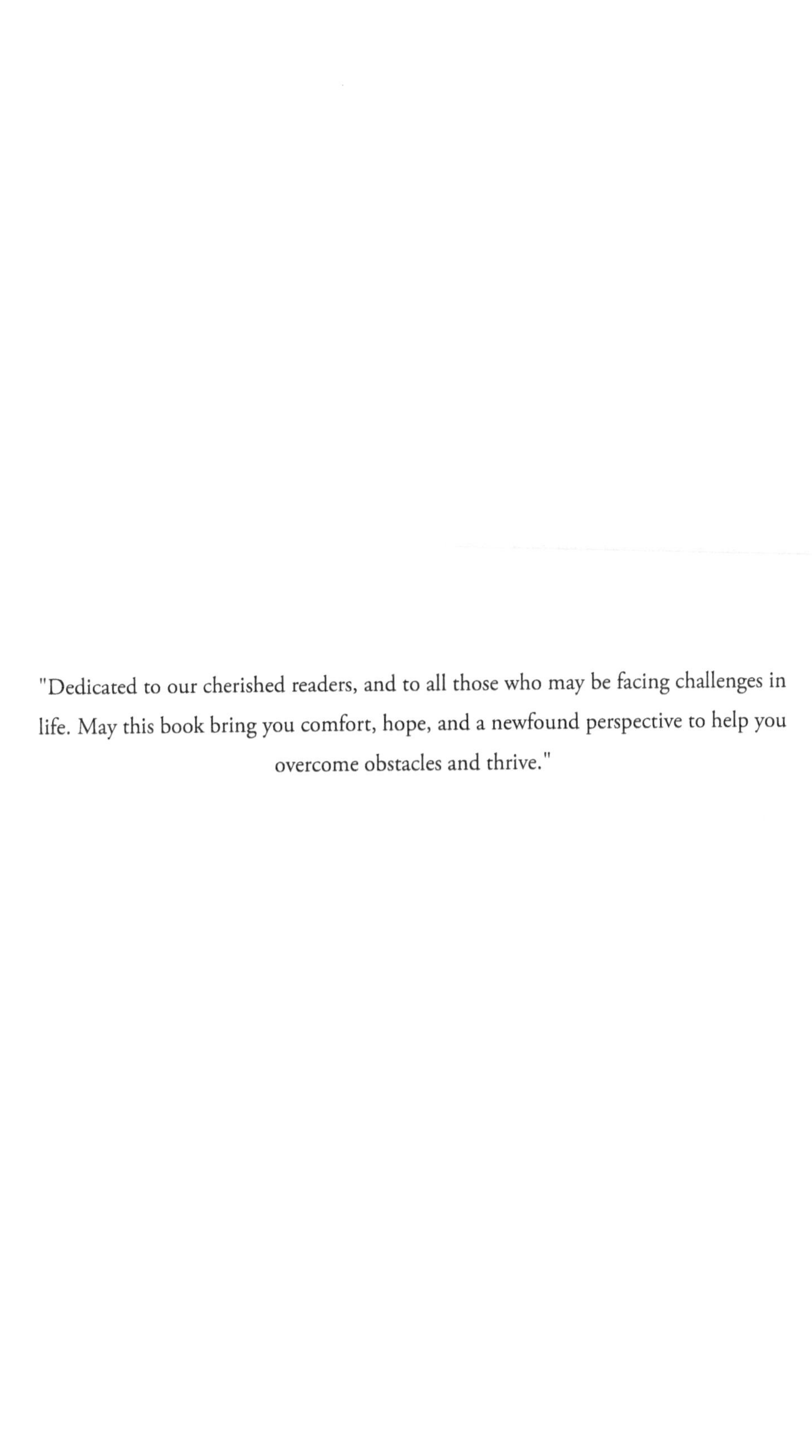

"Dedicated to our cherished readers, and to all those who may be facing challenges in life. May this book bring you comfort, hope, and a newfound perspective to help you overcome obstacles and thrive."

Contents

Foreword

"Discover the Depths of Humanity" is a fitting title for the seventh instalment in the "Homo Sapiens" series by Mawphniang Napoleon. This book promises to delve into the complexities of the human experience, offering new perspectives and illuminating insights. As a reader, you will be transported on a journey of self-discovery, exploring the intricacies of our species and gaining a deeper understanding of what it means to be human. With a body of work that includes thought-provoking titles such as "The Star's Illumination: A Quest for True Security" and "Thriving Amidst Adversity: The Burden of Avarice," Mawphniang Napoleon is a gifted author who has a unique ability to shed light on the human condition. So, be sure to read this book and the rest of the series, and discover the depths of humanity for yourself.

Preface

"Discover the Depths of Humanity"
A journey to the heart of what it means to be,
A quest for enlightenment, for clarity,
To delve into the complexities, to see
What lies beneath the surface, what we can be.
In this thought-provoking book by Mawphniang Napoleon,
We are offered new insights, a path to grow on,
To understand our species, to know
The depths of humanity, its ebb and flow.
With titles like "The Star's Illumination" and "Thriving Amidst Adversity,"
This insightful author has much to offer, you'll see,
So be sure to read this book, and the rest of the series,
And discover the depths of humanity, with ease.
In this journey, we will find what's true,
The essence of our being, our purpose, too,
So open this book, and let the journey begin,
And discover the depths of humanity within.
And as we delve deeper, we'll come to see,
The beauty and the struggle, the mystery,
Of being human, of living and breathing,
And all that it entails, the joys and grieving.
We'll explore the questions, the doubts and fears,
The triumphs and the failures, the laughter and tears,
And in the end, we'll come to know,
The depths of humanity, its highs and lows.
So let us embark on this journey together,
With open hearts and minds, and in good weather,
For the reward is great, the insights profound,

And the discoveries we'll make, will astound.

So come, and discover the depths of humanity,

With this thought-provoking book, by Mawphniang Napoleon's capability,

And be sure to read the rest of the series,

And other works by this insightful author, with ease.

A - Team

Acknowledgements

"Dear Readers,

We are grateful for your continued support and encouragement. Your passion for knowledge and thirst for understanding is what drives us to keep exploring new ideas and sharing our insights with you. Your eagerness to engage with our work is what motivates us to keep pushing the boundaries and reaching for new heights.

Your support has been invaluable, and we thank you for being a part of our journey. You have pushed us to be our best and to never stop learning. Your love for books and reading is what makes our work so meaningful, and we are honored to have you as our readers.

We hope that our work continues to inspire, challenge, and engage you. Thank you for being a part of our journey, and we look forward to continuing to share our insights with you in the future.

With gratitude,

Prologue

Welcome to "Discover the Depths of Humanity," the seventh instalment in the "Homo Sapiens" series by Mawphniang Napoleon. This thought-provoking book offers a unique perspective on the human experience, exploring the complexities of our species and providing new insights and enlightenment.

As you embark on this journey, you will delve into the intricacies of the human condition, gaining a deeper understanding of what it means to be human. You will be challenged to think beyond your current beliefs and to question the very essence of our existence.

Mawphniang Napoleon is a gifted author with a body of work that includes thought-provoking titles such as "The Star's Illumination: A Quest for True Security" and "Thriving Amidst Adversity: The Burden of Avarice." Their unique ability to shed light on the human experience has made them a sought-after voice in the literary world.

So, be sure to read this book and the rest of the "Homo Sapiens" series, as well as other works by this insightful author. Discover the depths of humanity for yourself and embark on a journey of self-discovery.

A - Team

1. The Star's Illumination: A Quest for True Security

In ancient times, when men were but mere mortals,
The concept of security was but a dream;
A fleeting thought, a wishful musing, a goal
That seemed as distant as the morning star.
Yet, as the ages passed and man evolved,
The quest for security became a quest for power.

Power, that elusive force that men desire,
Is but an illusion, a fleeting dream;
A mirage that promises eternal security,
But in reality, is but a fleeting goal.
For true security lies not in mortal power,
But in the wisdom of the ancient star.

The star, that beacon of hope in the night sky,
Guides men on their quest for security.
It shines with the wisdom of the ancient ones,
And reminds us that true power lies not in mortal might,
But in the balance of nature and the harmony of the dream.
For the star is a reminder of our ultimate goal.

The goal, that final destination we all seek,
Is not a place, but a state of being, a dream.
A dream of peace, of love, of security.

A dream that is within our reach, if we but follow the star.
For the star is the symbol of our ultimate goal,
And the key to unlocking our mortal power.

Power, that corrupting force that men desire,
Is but a fleeting thing, a mortal goal.
A goal that is ultimately empty, without security.
For true power lies not in mortal might,
But in the wisdom of the ancient star.
And it is only through the star that we can achieve our ultimate dream.

The dream, that final destination we all seek,
Is not a place, but a state of being, a dream.
A dream of peace, of love, of security.
A dream that is within our reach, if we but follow the star.
For the star is the symbol of our ultimate goal,
And the key to unlocking our mortal power.

Power, that corrupting force that men desire,
Is but a fleeting thing, a mortal goal.
A goal that is ultimately empty, without security.
For true power lies not in mortal might,
But in the wisdom of the ancient star.
And it is only through the star that we can achieve our ultimate dream.
The star is the key to our true security,
The guide that leads us to our ultimate goal.
For in the end, it is the dream that we all seek,
And it is the dream that we will all attain,
Through the wisdom of the ancient star,
And the power of our mortal souls.

And so, we embark on our journey,
To unlock the secrets of the ancient star,
And to uncover the wisdom of the ages.
For it is through this wisdom that we shall attain,
The true power of security and the dream.

The dream, that elusive state of being,
Is not a mere fantasy, but a reality.
A reality that can be reached through the star,
And the wisdom of the ancients.
For it is only through this wisdom that we shall attain,
The balance and harmony necessary for true security.

Security, that elusive state of being,
Is not a mere illusion, but a reality.
A reality that can be reached through the star,
And the wisdom of the ancients.
For it is only through this wisdom that we shall attain,
The peace and love necessary for the ultimate dream.

The dream, that final destination we all seek,
Is not a place, but a state of being, a dream.
A dream that is within our reach, if we but follow the star.
For the star is the symbol of our ultimate goal,
And the key to unlocking our true security.
And it is only through the star that we shall attain,
The wisdom of the ancients and the power of the dream.

The power of the dream, that elusive force,
Is not a mere fantasy, but a reality.
A reality that can be reached through the star,

And the wisdom of the ancients.
For it is only through this wisdom that we shall attain,
The true power of security and the ultimate dream.

The ultimate dream, that final destination we all seek,
Is not a place, but a state of being, a dream.
A dream that is within our reach, if we but follow the star.
For the star is the symbol of our ultimate goal,
And the key to unlocking our true security.
And it is only through the star that we shall attain,
The wisdom of the ancients and the power of the ultimate dream.

The ultimate dream, that state of being,
Is the ultimate goal, the ultimate security.
A security that can be reached through the star,
And the wisdom of the ancients.
For it is only through this wisdom that we shall attain,
The ultimate dream, the ultimate goal, the ultimate security.
For the ultimate dream is the ultimate goal,
And the ultimate security is the ultimate dream.
And it is only through the star that we shall attain,
The wisdom of the ancients, the ultimate dream and the ultimate security.

The ultimate dream and security, the ultimate goal,
Is the ultimate reality that we all seek.
A reality that is within our reach, if we but follow the star.
For the star is the symbol of our ultimate goal,
And the key to unlocking our true security.
And it is only through the star that we shall attain,
The wisdom of the ancients, the ultimate dream and the ultimate security.

The ultimate security, the ultimate dream, the ultimate goal,
Is the ultimate reality that we all seek.
A reality that is within our reach, if we but follow the star.
For the star is the symbol of our ultimate goal,
And the key to unlocking our true security.
And it is only through the star that we shall attain,
The wisdom of the ancients, the ultimate dream and the ultimate security.

The ultimate security, the ultimate dream, the ultimate goal,
Is the ultimate reality that we all seek.
A reality that is within our reach, if we but follow the star.
For the star is the symbol of our ultimate goal,
And the key to unlocking our true security.
And it is only through the star that we shall attain,
The wisdom of the ancients, the ultimate dream and the ultimate security.

But the star, it shines not for the unworthy,
For those who would seek to use its power for ill.
For the star is a beacon of truth and light,
Guiding us towards the ultimate goal,
But only if we are pure of heart and mind.
For the star will only reveal its secrets to the wise,
Those who have attained the wisdom of the ancients.

And the wisdom of the ancients, it is not easily gained,
But through study and contemplation, we shall attain.
For the ancients knew the secrets of the star,
And the power of the ultimate dream and security.
But their knowledge is not for the weak and lazy,
For only through hard work and dedication shall we unlock its secrets.

But once unlocked, the secrets of the star,
Shall lead us towards the ultimate goal,
For the star holds the key to ultimate security,
And the power of the ultimate dream.
And it is through the wisdom of the ancients,
That we shall attain this ultimate reality.

For the ultimate reality, it is not a dream,
But a state of being, attainable through the star.
For the star is the symbol of our ultimate goal,
And the key to unlocking our true security.
And it is only through the star that we shall attain,
The wisdom of the ancients, the ultimate dream and the ultimate security.

And so, we continue on our journey,
To unlock the secrets of the ancient star,
And to uncover the wisdom of the ages.
For it is through this wisdom that we shall attain,
The true power of security and the ultimate dream.
For the ultimate dream, the ultimate security,
Is the ultimate reality that we all seek,
And it is only through the star that we shall attain.

And yet, the journey is not without its perils,
For the star's secrets are guarded by the fates,
And the path to wisdom and security is fraught with challenges.
But the ancients knew this and left us with guidance,
For they too had to overcome obstacles to attain
Their ultimate goal of understanding the star.

Thus, we must not falter in our quest,

For the star's secrets are worth the trials.
We must be steadfast in our dedication,
For it is through perseverance that we shall attain
The ultimate dream and ultimate security.
We must trust in the wisdom of the ancients,
For they have laid the path before us.

But we must also remember that the ancients,
Though wise, were but human and subject to error.
Thus, we must also question and seek our own truth,
For the journey to the star's secrets is not one of blind faith.
It is through critical thinking and introspection that we shall attain
The ultimate goal, the ultimate dream, and ultimate security.

And so, we must balance the guidance of the ancients,
With our own intuition and understanding,
For it is through this balance that we shall attain
The ultimate goal, the ultimate dream, and ultimate security.
For the star's secrets are not only for the ancients,
But for all who seek wisdom and truth.

And as we unlock the secrets of the star,
We must also remember to share its wisdom,
For it is through sharing that we shall attain
The ultimate goal, the ultimate dream, and ultimate security.
For the star's light shines for all, not just the select few.

And so, we continue on our journey,
To unlock the secrets of the ancient star,
And to uncover the wisdom of the ages.
For it is through this wisdom that we shall attain,

The true power of security and the ultimate dream.
For the ultimate dream, the ultimate security,
Is the ultimate reality that we all seek,
And it is only through the star that we shall attain.

But as we strive towards the ultimate goal,
We must also be mindful of the consequences,
For the star's secrets hold great power,
And with great power comes great responsibility.
Thus, we must use the wisdom of the ancients,
To guide us towards a path of moral rectitude and security.

For the ultimate goal, the ultimate dream,
Is not only about attaining knowledge and power,
But also about using that knowledge for the betterment of all.
And it is through this moral compass,
That we shall truly attain the ultimate security,
For the ancients knew that true security,
Is not just about protection from harm,
But also about living in harmony with the world.

But the path towards true security,
Is not always a clear one,
And the ancients knew this,
For they too struggled with the weight of power and responsibility.
Thus, we must be humble in our quest,
For the ultimate goal, the ultimate dream,
Is not about personal gain,
But about the greater good.

And so, we continue on our journey,

To unlock the secrets of the ancient star,
And to uncover the wisdom of the ages.
For it is through this wisdom that we shall attain,
The true power of security and the ultimate dream.
But we must also remember,
That true attainment,
Is not just about reaching the ultimate goal,
But also about how we use that knowledge
and power to create a more secure and just world.

And so, we must tread carefully in our quest,
For the star's secrets hold the power of creation and destruction.
We must not let our desire for security,
Blind us to the potential consequences of our actions.
For the ancients knew that true security,
Is not just about protection from harm,
But also about maintaining balance in the world.

Thus, we must use the wisdom of the ancients,
As a guide to navigate the complexities of power and responsibility.
For the ultimate goal, the ultimate dream,
Is not just about attainment,
But also about stewardship and preservation.
And it is through this mindful approach,
That we shall truly attain the ultimate security,
For the ancients knew that true security,
Is not just about protecting the present,
But also about ensuring a secure future for all.

But the path towards true security,
Is not always an easy one,

For the ancients knew that progress and change,
Come at a cost and require sacrifice.
Thus, we must be willing to make difficult choices,
For the ultimate goal, the ultimate dream,
Is not about personal gain,
But about the greater good.

And so, we continue on our journey,
To unlock the secrets of the ancient star,
And to uncover the wisdom of the ages.
For it is through this wisdom that we shall attain,
The true power of security and the ultimate dream.
But we must also remember,
That true attainment,
Is not just about reaching the ultimate goal,
But also about how we use that knowledge and power to create a more secure and
just world,
For the ancients knew that true security,
Is not just about the present,
But also about the future.

But as we journey towards the ultimate goal,
We must also be wary of the dangers that lie ahead,
For the star's secrets hold great power,
And with great power comes great temptation.
Thus, we must guard against the pull of corruption,
And remain steadfast in our quest for true security.

For the ultimate goal, the ultimate dream,
Is not just about attainment of knowledge and power,
But also about using that knowledge for the betterment of all.

And it is through this moral fortitude,
That we shall truly attain the ultimate security,
For the ancients knew that true security,
Is not just about protection from harm,
But also about living in righteousness and integrity.

But the path towards true security,
Is not always a straightforward one,
And the ancients knew this,
For they too struggled with the allure of corruption and temptation.
Thus, we must be vigilant in our quest,
For the ultimate goal, the ultimate dream,
Is not about personal gain,
But about the greater good.

And so, we continue on our journey,
To unlock the secrets of the ancient star,
And to uncover the wisdom of the ages.
For it is through this wisdom that we shall attain,
The true power of security and the ultimate dream.
But we must also remember,
That true attainment,
Is not just about reaching the ultimate goal,
But also about how we use that knowledge
and power to create a more secure and just world,
For the ancients knew that true security,
Is not just about the present,
But also about the future and the eternal.
In trust doth man his fellow men impart
His secrets, hopes, and fears, with open heart
And trusting mind, that they may share the same

In bonds of trust, that none may e'er defame
The trust that holds them fast, a sacred flame
That burns within the soul, a guiding light

But trust is oft a fragile thing, a might
That waxes and wanes with each passing day
For trust is built upon the sands of time
And oft is shattered by the winds of change
And broken trust doth leave behind a blight

And yet, despite the fragility of trust
Man still doth seek it out, with open heart
For trust is vital to the human soul
It is the bond that keeps us from defame
And gives our lives a sense of purpose, a flame
That guides us through the darkness of our plight

But trust doth not just come from man alone
It is a force that flows through all of time
For trust is rooted deep within the earth
And doth sustain us, like the morning light
It is the trust in Nature's constant change
That allows us to weather every blight

And trust doth not just come from man alone
It also comes from science, a guiding light
That shows us how the world around us works
And helps us navigate through time and change
It is the trust in science's steady might
That allows us to conquer every plight

But trust doth not just come from man alone
It also comes from faith, a sacred flame
That gives us hope in times of darkest plight
And guides us through the trials of life
It is the trust in something greater than
Ourselves that allows us to transcend time

For trust is not just something we impart
But it is something that flows through all of life
It is a force that guides us through the dark
And gives us hope in times of greatest plight
It is the trust in ourselves, in others, and
In something greater, that gives us the might
To overcome all obstacles and defame
And keep the sacred flame of trust alight.

But trust doth not just come from faith alone
It also comes from knowledge, a guiding light
That shows us how to navigate through life
And helps us understand the mysteries of time
It is the trust in knowledge's steady might
That allows us to conquer every plight

But trust doth not just come from knowledge alone
It also comes from intuition, a sacred flame
That guides us through the twists and turns of life
And helps us make sense of the world around us
It is the trust in intuition's guiding light
That allows us to transcend every blight

But trust doth not just come from intuition alone

It also comes from reason, a steady might
That helps us make sense of the world around us
And navigate through the complexities of life
It is the trust in reason's guiding light
That allows us to overcome every plight

But trust doth not just come from reason alone
It also comes from experience, a sacred flame
That guides us through the trials of life
And helps us understand the mysteries of time
It is the trust in experience's guiding light
That allows us to transcend every blight

But trust doth not just come from experience alone
It also comes from imagination, a steady might
That helps us envision the world around us
And navigate through the unknowns of life
It is the trust in imagination's guiding light
That allows us to overcome every plight

But trust doth not just come from imagination alone
It also comes from the unknown, a sacred flame
That guides us through the mysteries of life
And helps us understand the secrets of time
It is the trust in the unknown's guiding light
That allows us to transcend every blight

For trust is not just something we impart
But it is something that flows through all of life
It is a force that guides us through the dark
And gives us hope in times of greatest plight

It is the trust in ourselves, in others, and
In the unknown, that gives us the might
To overcome all obstacles and defame
And keep the sacred flame of trust alight.

But trust doth not just come from the unknown alone
It also comes from the past, a guiding light
That shows us the lessons of history
And helps us avoid the mistakes of time
It is the trust in the past's steady might
That allows us to conquer every plight

But trust doth not just come from the past alone
It also comes from the present, a sacred flame
That guides us through the challenges of life
And helps us make the most of every moment
It is the trust in the present's guiding light
That allows us to transcend every blight

But trust doth not just come from the present alone
It also comes from the future, a steady might
That helps us plan and dream for what is to come
And navigate through the unknowns of life
It is the trust in the future's guiding light
That allows us to overcome every plight

But trust doth not just come from the future alone
It also comes from the self, a sacred flame
That guides us through the journey of life
And helps us understand our own nature
It is the trust in the self's guiding light

That allows us to transcend every blight

But trust doth not just come from the self alone
It also comes from the divine, a steady might
That helps us connect to something greater
And navigate through the mysteries of life
It is the trust in the divine's guiding light
That allows us to overcome every plight

For trust is not just something we impart
But it is something that flows through all of life
It is a force that guides us through the dark
And gives us hope in times of greatest plight
It is the trust in ourselves, in others, and
In the divine, that gives us the might
To overcome all obstacles and defame
And keep the sacred flame of trust alight.

But trust doth not just come from the divine alone
It also comes from the natural world, a guiding light
That shows us the beauty and power of the earth
And helps us understand the balance of time
It is the trust in the natural world's steady might
That allows us to conquer every plight

But trust doth not just come from the natural world alone
It also comes from society, a sacred flame
That guides us through the complexities of life
And helps us make sense of the human condition
It is the trust in society's guiding light
That allows us to transcend every blight

But trust doth not just come from society alone
It also comes from technology, a steady might
That helps us advance and improve our lives
And navigate through the unknowns of the future
It is the trust in technology's guiding light
That allows us to overcome every plight

But trust doth not just come from technology alone
It also comes from art, a sacred flame
That guides us through the emotional landscape of life
And helps us understand the human experience
It is the trust in art's guiding light
That allows us to transcend every blight

But trust doth not just come from art alone
It also comes from science, a steady might
That helps us understand the workings of the world
And navigate through the mysteries of existence
It is the trust in science's guiding light
That allows us to overcome every plight

For trust is not just something we impart
But it is something that flows through all of life
It is a force that guides us through the dark
And gives us hope in times of greatest plight
It is the trust in ourselves, in others, and
In the natural world, society, technology, art,
and science, that gives us the might
To overcome all obstacles and defame
And keep the sacred flame of trust alight.

But trust doth not just come from science alone
It also comes from faith, a guiding light
That shows us the path to spiritual enlightenment
And helps us understand the mysteries of divine
It is the trust in faith's steady might
That allows us to conquer every plight

But trust doth not just come from faith alone
It also comes from relationships, a sacred flame
That guides us through the connections of life
And helps us build trust in one another
It is the trust in relationships' guiding light
That allows us to transcend every blight

But trust doth not just come from relationships alone
It also comes from tradition, a steady might
That helps us understand the past and its impact on the present
And navigate through the customs of life
It is the trust in tradition's guiding light
That allows us to overcome every plight

But trust doth not just come from tradition alone
It also comes from innovation, a sacred flame
That guides us through the progress of life
And helps us break free from the status quo
It is the trust in innovation's guiding light
That allows us to transcend every blight

But trust doth not just come from innovation alone
It also comes from logic and reason, a steady might

That helps us make sense of the world and question what we know
And navigate through the complexities of life
It is the trust in logic and reason's guiding light
That allows us to overcome every plight

For trust is not just something we impart
But it is something that flows through all of life
It is a force that guides us through the dark
And gives us hope in times of greatest plight
It is the trust in ourselves, in others, and
In faith, relationships, tradition, innovation,
logic, and reason, that gives us the might
To overcome all obstacles and defame
And keep the sacred flame of trust alight.

But trust doth not just come from logic and reason alone
It also comes from intuition, a guiding light
That shows us the path to inner wisdom
And helps us understand the mysteries of the mind
It is the trust in intuition's steady might
That allows us to conquer every plight

But trust doth not just come from intuition alone
It also comes from empathy, a sacred flame
That guides us through the emotions of life
And helps us build trust in one another
It is the trust in empathy's guiding light
That allows us to transcend every blight

But trust doth not just come from empathy alone
It also comes from resilience, a steady might

That helps us overcome the challenges of life
And navigate through the hardships of existence
It is the trust in resilience's guiding light
That allows us to overcome every plight

But trust doth not just come from resilience alone
It also comes from creativity, a sacred flame
That guides us through the expression of life
And helps us see the world in a new light
It is the trust in creativity's guiding light
That allows us to transcend every blight

But trust doth not just come from creativity alone
It also comes from critical thinking, a steady might
That helps us question the status quo and seek truth
And navigate through the complexities of life
It is the trust in critical thinking's guiding light
That allows us to overcome every plight

For trust is not just something we impart
But it is something that flows through all of life
It is a force that guides us through the dark
And gives us hope in times of greatest plight
It is the trust in ourselves, in others, and
In intuition, empathy, resilience, creativity,
and critical thinking, that gives us the might
To overcome all obstacles and defame
And keep the sacred flame of trust alight.

But trust doth not just come from critical thinking alone
It also comes from self-reflection, a guiding light

That shows us the path to self-discovery
And helps us understand the mysteries of the soul
It is the trust in self-reflection's steady might
That allows us to conquer every plight

But trust doth not just come from self-reflection alone
It also comes from self-awareness, a sacred flame
That guides us through the journey of life
And helps us build trust in one's self
It is the trust in self-awareness's guiding light
That allows us to transcend every blight

But trust doth not just come from self-awareness alone
It also comes from self-discipline, a steady might
That helps us overcome the temptations of life
And navigate through the struggles of self-control
It is the trust in self-discipline's guiding light
That allows us to overcome every plight

But trust doth not just come from self-discipline alone
It also comes from self-compassion, a sacred flame
That guides us through the hardships of life
And helps us see the beauty in our faults
It is the trust in self-compassion's guiding light
That allows us to transcend every blight

But trust doth not just come from self-compassion alone
It also comes from self-acceptance, a steady might
That helps us embrace our true selves and find peace
And navigate through the complexities of life
It is the trust in self-acceptance's guiding light

That allows us to overcome every plight

For trust is not just something we impart
But it is something that flows through all of life
It is a force that guides us through the dark
And gives us hope in times of greatest plight
It is the trust in ourselves, in others, and
In self-reflection, self-awareness, self-discipline,
self-compassion, and self-acceptance, that gives us the might
To overcome all obstacles and defame
And keep the sacred flame of trust alight.

But trust doth not just come from self-acceptance alone
It also comes from forgiveness, a guiding light
That shows us the path to inner peace
And helps us understand the complexities of the heart
It is the trust in forgiveness's steady might
That allows us to conquer every plight

But trust doth not just come from forgiveness alone
It also comes from humility, a sacred flame
That guides us through the journey of life
And helps us build trust in our fellow man
It is the trust in humility's guiding light
That allows us to transcend every blight

But trust doth not just come from humility alone
It also comes from gratitude, a steady might
That helps us overcome the trials of life
And navigate through the storms of fate
It is the trust in gratitude's guiding light

That allows us to overcome every plight

But trust doth not just come from gratitude alone
It also comes from kindness, a sacred flame
That guides us through the hardships of life
And helps us see the goodness in the world
It is the trust in kindness's guiding light
That allows us to transcend every blight

But trust doth not just come from kindness alone
It also comes from integrity, a steady might
That helps us stand for what is right and true
And navigate through the complexities of life
It is the trust in integrity's guiding light
That allows us to overcome every plight

For trust is not just something we impart
But it is something that flows through all of life
It is a force that guides us through the dark
And gives us hope in times of greatest plight
It is the trust in ourselves, in others, and
In forgiveness, humility, gratitude, kindness, and integrity, that gives us the might
To overcome all obstacles and defame
And keep the sacred flame of trust alight.

But trust doth not just come from integrity alone
It also comes from empathy, a guiding light
That shows us the path to understanding others
And helps us understand the complexities of the human mind
It is the trust in empathy's steady might
That allows us to conquer every plight

But trust doth not just come from empathy alone
It also comes from compassion, a sacred flame
That guides us through the journey of life
And helps us build trust in our fellow man
It is the trust in compassion's guiding light
That allows us to transcend every blight

But trust doth not just come from compassion alone
It also comes from patience, a steady might
That helps us overcome the trials of life
And navigate through the storms of fate
It is the trust in patience's guiding light
That allows us to overcome every plight

But trust doth not just come from patience alone
It also comes from perseverance, a sacred flame
That guides us through the hardships of life
And helps us see the beauty in persevering
It is the trust in perseverance's guiding light
That allows us to transcend every blight

But trust doth not just come from perseverance alone
It also comes from courage, a steady might
That helps us face our fears and overcome them
And navigate through the complexities of life
It is the trust in courage's guiding light
That allows us to overcome every plight

For trust is not just something we impart
But it is something that flows through all of life

It is a force that guides us through the dark
And gives us hope in times of greatest plight
It is the trust in ourselves, in others, and
In empathy, compassion, patience, perseverance, and courage, that gives us the
might
To overcome all obstacles and defame
And keep the sacred flame of trust alight.

2. The Determinism Dilemma

In the realm of science and philosophy,
Determinism is a subject of great depth,
For it raises questions of free will and fate,
And the nature of causality in our state.

Is our destiny predetermined,
Or do we have the power to choose,
To shape our lives with our own hands,
And forge our own path, with no excuse?

The determinists argue that all events,
Are causally linked in a chain,
That the past and present determine the future,
And our actions are predetermined, without refrain.

But the problem of free will arises,
For if all is predetermined, how can we be free,
To make our own choices and decisions,
And shape our own destiny?

The philosophers debate,
While scientists seek to understand,
The nature of causality and time,
And the complex web of cause and effect that spans.

But perhaps the answer lies,

In a combination of both views,
For while the past and present may shape the future,
Our choices and actions still play a role, it's true.

So let us not despair,
For though determinism may seem strict,
We still have the power to shape our own fate,
And make our own path, with every tick-tock.

But what of those who argue,
That free will is but an illusion,
That our choices are not truly our own,
But predetermined by some unseen fusion.

They point to the laws of physics,
And the workings of the brain,
As evidence for this viewpoint,
And claim that free will is in vain.

But is this not a paradox,
For if we are truly predetermined,
How can we be held responsible,
For actions that were preordained?

And yet, even with this understanding,
We cannot simply give up our fight,
For even if our choices are limited,
We still have the power to choose what is right.

For determinism may be the rule,
But within that rule, there is still room,

For us to make our own choices,
And pave our own way, with our own broom.

So let us not be discouraged,
By the idea of determinism,
For while it may limit our choices,
It does not limit our ability to make them.

For in the end, it is not the fate that is predetermined,
But the way we choose to react to it,
And that, my friends, is truly where our power lies,
The power of free will, the power of wit.

But what of the future,
Is it truly set in stone?
Do our choices and actions,
Really determine where we'll be shown?

The concept of determinism,
Can be both liberating and confining,
For it may give us a sense of purpose,
But it can also leave us feeling binding.

For if our future is predetermined,
Does it not take away the need to strive,
But if we take control of our fate,
Does it not make life more alive?

Perhaps the answer lies,
In the balance between the two,
For determinism can give us direction,

But free will allows us to pursue.

So let us not be discouraged,
By the idea of determinism,
For while it may shape our future,
It does not limit our ability to make the most of it.

Let us embrace the power of free will,
And strive to make the most of our fate,
For in the end, it is not the destination,
But the journey that truly makes life great.

Determinism may be a complex subject,
But it is one that is worth exploring,
For it can bring us a sense of understanding,
And open our eyes to the possibilities of living.

But perhaps the ultimate truth,
Is that determinism and free will,
Are not mutually exclusive,
But rather, they coexist still.

For in the grand scheme of things,
The universe follows its own laws,
But within that, we have the power,
To make choices and shape our own cause.

So let us not despair,
For the idea of determinism,
For it is not a prison,
But a tool for understanding, and wisdom.

Let us strive to make the most,
Of the choices that we have,
And let us remember,
That we are not mere slaves,

Of fate or destiny,
But rather, masters of our own fate,
For even if the future is predetermined,
We have the power to make it great.

So let us embrace determinism,
As a guide for our journey,
And let us use our free will,
To make the most of our life story.

For in the end, it is not the fate that is predetermined,
But the way we choose to react to it,
And that, my friends, is truly where our power lies,
The power of free will, the power of wit.

But as we ponder these complex questions,
We must not forget to consider,
The role of randomness and chance,
In shaping our lives, forever.

For even if our future is predetermined,
There is still room for the unexpected,
For the events that we cannot control,
And the opportunities that we must respect it.

So let us not be fooled,
Into thinking that we have complete control,
For there will always be a certain degree,
Of uncertainty, in life's ultimate goal.

But this does not mean,
That we should give up our fight,
For even with the unknown,
We can still make things right.

For in the end, it is not just about,
Determinism or free will,
But about how we navigate,
The unpredictable, the unknown thrill.

So let us embrace,
The beauty of the unexpected,
For it is in the unknown,
That we find the true meaning of life, the selected.

In conclusion, determinism is a complex subject,
That raises many questions,
But let us remember that it is not the only factor,
That shapes our lives, and our decisions.

For while determinism may guide us,
Free will and randomness also play a role,
In the journey of our lives,
And the path that we must stroll.

And as we journey through life,

We must not forget the role of perception,
In shaping our understanding,
Of the world, and our own self-reflection.

For even if our fate is predetermined,
The way we perceive it,
Can greatly impact our actions,
And the way we react to it.

So let us not be slaves,
To a rigid understanding of fate,
But rather open our minds,
And allow for a nuanced perspective, to take.

For in the end, it is not just about,
Determinism or free will,
But about how we interpret,
The world, and our own will.

So let us embrace,
The power of perspective,
For it is in our own perception,
That we find true freedom, and connection.

In conclusion, determinism is a complex subject,
That raises many questions,
But let us remember that it is not the only factor,
That shapes our lives, and our decisions.

For while determinism may guide us,
Free will, randomness and perception also play a role,

MAWPHNIANG NAPOLEON

In the journey of our lives,
And the path that we must stroll.

But as we delve deeper,
Into the intricacies of determinism,
We must not forget the role of ethics,
In shaping our actions and decisions.

For even if our fate is predetermined,
The way we choose to act,
Can greatly impact not only our own lives,
But also the lives of those around us, in fact.

So let us not be slaves,
To a predetermined path,
But rather strive to make the most,
Of the choices that we have.

For in the end, it is not just about,
Determinism or free will,
But about how we use them,
To make the world a better place, to fulfill.

So let us embrace,
The power of ethics,
For it is in our actions,
That we find true purpose, and ethics.

So let us embrace the complexity of determinism,
And use it as a tool,

To better understand ourselves,
And the world, in a more holistic and ethical school.

But as we ponder the complexities,
Of determinism and free will,
We must not forget the role of consciousness,
In shaping our understanding, and thrill.

For even if our fate is predetermined,
The way we experience it,
Can greatly impact our actions,
And the way we react to it.

So let us not be slaves,
To a predetermined path,
But rather strive to make the most,
Of the experiences that we have.

For in the end, it is not just about,
Determinism or free will,
But about how we perceive and experience,
The world, and our own will.

But as we delve deeper,
Into the intricacies of determinism,
We must not forget the role of evolution,
In shaping our actions and decisions.

For even if our fate is predetermined,
The way we adapt and evolve,
Can greatly impact not only our own lives,

But also the lives of those around us, and more.

So let us not be slaves,
To a predetermined path,
But rather strive to make the most,
Of the opportunities that we have.

For in the end, it is not just about,
Determinism or free will,
But about how we use them,
To evolve and adapt, and fulfill.

So let us embrace,
The power of evolution,
For it is in our ability to adapt,
That we find true purpose, and evolution.

Determinism is a complex subject,
That raises many questions,
But let us remember that it is not the only factor,
That shapes our lives, and our decisions.

For while determinism may guide us,
Free will, randomness, perception, ethics, consciousness and evolution also play a
role,
In the journey of our lives,
And the path that we must stroll.

So let us embrace the complexity of determinism,
And use it as a tool,
To better understand ourselves,

And the world, in a more holistic, ethical, conscious, and evolutionary school.

And as we journey through life,
With the understanding of determinism,
We must not forget the role of culture,
In shaping our actions and decisions.

For even if our fate is predetermined,
The way we are influenced by culture,
Can greatly impact not only our own lives,
But also the lives of those around us, and the nature.

So let us not be slaves,
To a predetermined path,
But rather strive to make the most,
Of the cultural influences that we have.

It is not just about,
Determinism or free will,
But about how we use them,
To navigate the cultural realm, and fulfill.

For while determinism may guide us,
Free will, randomness, perception, ethics, consciousness, evolution and culture also
play a role,
In the journey of our lives,
And the path that we must stroll.

So let us embrace the complexity of determinism,
And use it as a tool,
To better understand ourselves,

And the world, in a more holistic, ethical, conscious, evolutionary, and cultural
school.

As we delve deeper,
Into the intricacies of determinism,
We must not forget the role of spirituality,
In shaping our actions and decisions.

For even if our fate is predetermined,
The way we connect with the spiritual realm,
Can greatly impact not only our own lives,
But also the way we understand our place in the world and its helm.

So let us not be slaves,
To a predetermined path,
But rather strive to make the most,
Of the spiritual insights and guidance we have.

For in the end, it is not just about,
Determinism or free will,
But about how we use them,
To connect with the spiritual realm, and fulfill.

So let us embrace,
The power of spirituality,
For it is in our ability to understand and connect with the divine,
That we find true purpose, and spirituality.

Determinism is a complex subject,
That raises many questions,
But let us remember that it is not the only factor,

That shapes our lives, and our decisions.

For while determinism may guide us,
Free will, randomness, perception, ethics, consciousness, evolution, culture and
spirituality also play a role,
In the journey of our lives,
And the path that we must stroll.

So let us embrace the complexity of determinism,
And use it as a tool,
To better understand ourselves,
And the world, in a more holistic, ethical, conscious, evolutionary, cultural and
spiritual school.

As we journey through life,
With the understanding of determinism,
We must not forget the role of imagination,
In shaping our actions and decisions.

For even if our fate is predetermined,
The way we use our imagination,
Can greatly impact not only our own lives,
But also the way we view the world and its formation.

So let us not be slaves,
To a predetermined path,
But rather strive to make the most,
Of the creative potential that we have.

For in the end, it is not just about,
Determinism or free will,

But about how we use them,
To unleash our imagination, and fulfill.

So let us embrace,
The power of imagination,
For it is in our ability to think creatively,
That we find true innovation, and imagination.

Determinism is a complex subject,
That raises many questions,
But let us remember that it is not the only factor,
That shapes our lives, and our decisions.

For while determinism may guide us,
Free will, randomness, perception, ethics, consciousness, evolution, culture,
spirituality and imagination also play a role,
In the journey of our lives,
And the path that we must stroll.

So let us embrace the complexity of determinism,
And use it as a tool,
To better understand ourselves,
And the world, in a more holistic, ethical, conscious, evolutionary, cultural,
spiritual, and imaginative school.

As we delve deeper,
Into the intricacies of determinism,
We must not forget the role of emotions,
In shaping our actions and decisions.

For even if our fate is predetermined,

The way we experience and express emotions,
Can greatly impact not only our own lives,
But also the way we interact with others, and the way we cope with the notions.

So let us not be slaves,
To a predetermined path,
But rather strive to make the most,
Of the emotional intelligence that we have.

For in the end, it is not just about,
Determinism or free will,
But about how we use them,
To navigate the emotional realm, and fulfill.

So let us embrace,
The power of emotions,
For it is in our ability to understand, express and regulate them,
That we find true fulfillment and connection, and emotions.

As we journey through life,
With the understanding of determinism,
We must not forget the role of technology,
In shaping our actions and decisions.

For even if our fate is predetermined,
The way we use and interact with technology,
Can greatly impact not only our own lives,
But also the way we interact with others, and the way we perceive the reality.

So let us not be slaves,
To a predetermined path,

But rather strive to make the most,
Of the technological advancements that we have.

For in the end, it is not just about,
Determinism or free will,
But about how we use them,
To navigate the technological realm, and fulfill.

And the path that we must stroll.

So let us embrace the complexity of determinism,
And use it as a tool,
To better understand ourselves,
And the world, in a more holistic, ethical, conscious, evolutionary, cultural,
spiritual, imaginative, emotional and technological school.

As we navigate the ever-changing landscape,
Of our modern world,
Let us remember the importance,
Of considering all these factors, in our quest for understanding and unfurled.

For only by embracing the complexity,
Of determinism and all its layers,
Can we truly understand,
The world and our place in it, and its players.

So let us not be afraid,
To question and explore,
For in the pursuit of knowledge,
We will find true wisdom and more.

For even if our fate is predetermined,
We still have the power,
To shape our own destiny,
And make the most of every hour.

So let us embrace determinism,
As a guide on our journey,
And let us use our free will,
To make the most of our life's story.

And as we move forward,
On our journey through life,
Let us remember that determinism,
Is not the end, but the start of the strife.

For while it may guide us,
It is not the only force at play,
And it is up to us,
To make the most of our own way.

Let us not be discouraged,
By the idea of predetermined fate,
For it is in the choices we make,
That our true power lies, and its mate.

Let us strive to make the most,
Of the opportunities before us,
And let us remember,
That we are not mere slaves, but the trust.

For even if our fate is predetermined,

We still have the ability to shape,
Our own destiny, and make the most,
Of every moment, and its cape.

So let us embrace determinism,
As a guide on our journey,
And let us use our free will,
To make the most of our life's story.

It is not the fate that is predetermined,
But the way we choose to react to it,
And that, my friends, is truly where our power lies,
The power of free will, the power to make the most of it.

And as we continue on our journey,
Through the vast expanse of time,
Let us remember that determinism,
Is not the end, but a marker of our climb.

For while it may guide us,
It is not the only force at play,
And it is up to us,
To find our own unique way.

Let us not be discouraged,
By the idea of predetermined fate,
For it is in the choices we make,
That our true strength lies, and its weight.

Let us strive to make the most,
Of the opportunities before us,

And let us remember,
That we are not mere puppets, but the trust.

For even if our fate is predetermined,
We still have the ability to shape,
Our own destiny, and make the most,
Of every moment, and its drape.

So let us embrace determinism,
As a guide on our journey,
And let us use our free will,
To make the most of our life's story.

For in the end, it is not the fate that is predetermined,
But the way we choose to react to it,
And that, my friends, is truly where our power lies,
The power of free will, the power to make the most of it.

So let us not be limited by determinism,
But let us use it as a tool,
To navigate our journey,
And make the most of every rule.

3. The Phoenix's Journey : Rejection's Remedy

Rejection, a plight that oft doth sting,
A wound that cuts deep, a heart's painful ring.
A bitter pill, a thorn in one's side,
A feeling that oft doth one's spirit deride.

But what is this thing, this rejection so cruel,
That strikes without warning, that makes one a fool?
Is it a force of nature, a cosmic decree,
Or a mere construct, a product of humanity?

Some say it's a test, a trial by fire,
A means to build strength, to one's spirit aspire.
Others claim it's a curse, a fate most dire,
A sign of one's failure, a harbinger of mire.

But perhaps it's a lesson, a chance to learn,
A way to grow, one's perspective to turn.
An opportunity to see the world anew,
To find one's true self, and one's purpose to pursue.

For rejection is not an end, but a start,
A chance to break free, and to play a new part.
It's not a defeat, but a chance to prevail,
A test of one's will, and one's spirit to unveil.

So when rejection comes, and it oft doth,
Remember this truth, and let it guide you.
For it's not the end, but a new beginning,
A chance to rise up, and to victory's winning.

And as one rises from the ashes,
A phoenix reborn, with newfound passes,
One must not forget, the rejection's role,
For it has played its part, in making one whole.

For without the rejection, one may not know,
The strength that lies within, the fire that doth glow.
One may not see, the potential that's there,
The dreams that can be reached, the love that can be shared.

So let us embrace the rejection,
As a stepping stone, towards perfection.
Let us not fear, the sting of its might,
For it is in the darkest of nights,

That the stars shine brightest,
And the soul finds its lightest.
For rejection is not the end,
But a new chapter, to pen.

And in that chapter, we shall write,
Of our journey, our struggles, and our fight.
For in the end, it is not the rejection,
But the way we face it, that earns us recognition.

So let us not cower, in the face of rejection,
But rise up and embrace it with conviction.
For it is in the rejection, that we truly grow,
And in that growth, our true selves, we shall know.

And as we journey on this mortal plane,
We may come across rejection again and again.
But we must not let it break our stride,
For it is only through rejection, that we can abide.

By the test of life, and emerge victorious,
With a heart of steel, and a spirit auspicious.
For rejection is not the end, but a new path,
A chance to rise up, and to break the aftermath.

Of our fears and doubts, that once held us back,
And to embrace the unknown, without a lack.
For it is in the unknown, that we truly grow,
And find our purpose, and our destiny bestow.

So let us not fear rejection,
But embrace it with open arms, and with affection.
For it is through rejection, that we evolve,
And find the strength, to rise above and resolve.

So let us not be afraid, to be rejected,
But let us be brave, and let our light be reflected.
For in the end, it is not the rejection,
But the way we face it, that earns us true redemption.

For rejection is not the end, but a new beginning,

A chance for growth, and for self-refining.
It is a test, of our strength and our will,
And a chance to rise above, and to conquer still.

It is a challenge, to our very core,
A test of our resolve, and what we truly adore.
For in the face of rejection, we must not falter,
But rise above, and let our true selves alter.

To be better, to be stronger, to be bolder,
To reach for the stars, and to break the molder.
For rejection is not the end, but a new door,
A chance to evolve, and to explore.

The depths of our being, and the heights of our dreams,
To reach for the stars, and to accomplish it seems.
So let us not fear rejection, but embrace it,
For it is through rejection, that true success is met.

For in the end, it is not the rejection, but the way we face it,
That defines us, and makes us who we truly are, and our spirit to cherish it.

Thus, let us not be afraid, to face rejection head-on,
But let us be brave, and our true selves to be shown.
For in the face of rejection, we must not retreat,
But rise above, and our true selves to meet.

For rejection is not the end, but a new chapter,
A chance to grow, and to become a better capture.
It is a test, of our resilience and our grit,
And a chance to emerge stronger, from the pits.

It is a challenge, to our very essence,
A test of our mettle, and our true presence.
For in the face of rejection, we must not waver,
But rise above, and our true selves to discover.

So let us not fear rejection, but embrace it,
For it is through rejection, that we truly fit.

4. The Vital Essence: A Metaphor of Blood

Blood, the vital fluid that courses through our veins,
A metaphor for life, with many intricate pains.
It flows with purpose, to nourish and sustain,
A delicate balance, that must always remain.

But blood is not just a physical thing,
It's also a symbol, of our deepest being.
It represents the bond that connects us all,
The ties that bind, that make us stand tall.

Blood is the thread that weaves through our history,
The source of our strength and our mystery.
It tells the story of who we are,
A reflection of our deepest scars.

In blood we find the essence of our existence,
A reminder of our fragile persistence.
It is the bond that unites us in life,
A metaphor for the struggles and strife.

But even as it flows, it also reminds,
Of the transience of all mortal kinds,
For in the end, it will return to the earth,
A reminder of our own fragile birth.

So let us cherish the blood that runs through our veins,
A metaphor for life, with all its pains and gains,
For it is in this fluid, that we truly live,
A reminder of the beauty, and the power it gives.

Blood, it is the life force that animates,
A symphony of cells, that pulsates and dictates.
It is the river that runs through our being,
A metaphor for the journey, that we are seeing.

With every beat of our hearts, blood flows,
A symbol of the journey, that everyone goes.
It is the link that connects us to one another,
A reminder of the ties, that we can't sever.

Blood is the bond that connects us to our past,
It is the legacy, that will forever last.
It tells the story of our ancestors,
A reminder of the sacrifices, they made for us.

But blood is not just a metaphor, it's also a fact,
It is the substance that keeps us alive, in tact.
It is the carrier of oxygen, and nutrients,
A reminder of the importance, of science and its fruits.

So let us honor the blood that runs through our veins,
A metaphor for life, with all its pains and gains.
It is the fluid, that gives us the gift of being,
A reminder of the beauty, and the power it brings.

Blood, it is the river of life that never stops flowing,
A symbol of our existence, that is always growing.
It is the force that keeps us moving forward,
A reminder of the beauty, that is always in store.

Blood is the link that connects us to the future,
A symbol of the possibilities, that are yet to suture.
It is the conduit of hope, and aspiration,
A reminder of the dreams, that we are chasing after.

But blood is not just a metaphor, it's also a symbol,
It is the reminder of the sacrifice, that is so vital.
It is the sacrifice that is made for love and for family,
A reminder of the importance of community.

So let us remember the blood that runs through our veins,
A metaphor for life, with all its pains and gains.
It is the fluid that keeps us alive, and united,
A reminder of the beauty, and the power of life.

Blood, it is the elixir of life that keeps us going,
A metaphor for the journey, that is always flowing.
It is the force that drives us to be better,
A reminder of the beauty, that we can treasure.

Blood is the link that connects us to our purpose,
A symbol of the meaning, that we must uncover.
It is the fuel that powers our aspirations,
A reminder of the goals, that we must chase with persistence.

But blood is not just a metaphor, it's also a reminder,

Of the fragility of life, and the struggles we must surmount.
It is the sacrifice that we must make, to live fully,
A reminder of the importance of taking action, and being fully.

So let us value the blood that runs through our veins,
A metaphor for life, with all its pains and gains.
It is the fluid that gives us the gift of being alive,
A reminder of the beauty, and the power of life, that we must thrive.

Blood, it is the river of life that never dries,
A metaphor for the journey, that never dies.
It is the force that keeps us going, and strong,
A reminder of the beauty, that we must prolong.

Blood is the link that connects us to our humanity,
A symbol of the empathy, that we must carry.
It is the bond that unites us in our diversity,
A reminder of the importance, of unity and charity.

But blood is not just a metaphor, it's also a call,
To action, to work towards a better world for all.
It is the sacrifice that we make, for peace and justice,
A reminder of the importance of making a difference.

So let us cherish the blood that runs through our veins,
A metaphor for life, with all its pains and gains.
It is the fluid that gives us the gift of being alive,
A reminder of the beauty, and the power of life, that we must strive.

Blood, it is the river of life that flows within,
A metaphor for the journey, that never ends.

It is the force that keeps us moving, and alive,
A reminder of the beauty, that we must survive.

Blood is the link that connects us to our emotions,
A symbol of the feelings, that we must control or own them.
It is the bond that unites us in our passions,
A reminder of the importance, of living with compassion.

But blood is not just a metaphor, it's also a test,
To check our strength and courage, to face life's quest.
It is the sacrifice that we make, to grow and evolve,
A reminder of the importance of self-improvement and resolve.

So let us respect the blood that runs through our veins,
A metaphor for life, with all its pains and gains.
It is the fluid that gives us the gift of being alive,
A reminder of the beauty, and the power of life, that we must thrive.

Blood, it is the river of life that flows within,
A metaphor for the journey, that never ends.
It is the force that gives us life, and vitality,
A reminder of the beauty, that we must constantly rely

5. The Paradox of Shame

Or doth true freedom lie in finding balance
Between the self and others, and reconciling
The need for self-expression and preservation,
And the need for social harmony and cooperation?
For shame, though oft a burden, doth have purpose:
To guide us towards a better, nobler way,
And make us strive for self-improvement, else
We'd sink into depravity and vice.
But in embracing shame, we must not let
It control us completely, and forget
The beauty of self-expression and the worth
Of being true to one's self, and not just conforming
To society's ideals, for that doth make
Us lose our unique humanity, and dull
Our shining inner light. So let us strive
To find the balance, and not let shame control our lives.
But what of those who have been wronged and shamed,
Their innocence tarnished by false accusations?
How can they find redemption and regain
Their sense of self-worth, and shed the weight
Of shame that was not rightfully their own?
Perchance, through forgiveness and understanding,
Both of self and of others, they can find release
From the shackles of false shame and move forward,
Embracing their true selves and not conforming
To the judgment of those who wronged them. For true
Freedom lies in self-acceptance and self-love.
And yet, the path towards redemption is not easy,
For oft times, the wounds of shame run deep,
And healing takes time and effort. But with determination
And support from loved ones, one can rise above

The shame imposed upon them, and reclaim
Their sense of self-worth and dignity.
For shame, though oft a burden, can also be a teacher,
Showing us where we have wronged and where we can improve.
But it is important to remember that true shame
Is rooted in one's actions and not in one's being.
So let us strive to separate the two, and not let
The weight of false shame control our lives.
Shame is a complex emotion,
With both positive and negative effects on the soul.
But through self-reflection, forgiveness, and balance,
We can learn to embrace shame as a teacher,
And not let it control us, but rather guide us
Towards a nobler and more fulfilling existence
And as we journey through this ever-changing world,
Let us remember that shame is not a constant,
But an emotion that shifts and evolves,
With different meanings and causes in different cultures,
And even within the same person, depending on the context.
Thus, it's important to approach it with an open mind,
And not to stereotype or generalize the experience of shame.
Additionally, we must recognize the power dynamics
That often underlie shame, and acknowledge that certain individuals
Are more likely to be shamed and stigmatized based on their race, gender,
Sexual orientation, socioeconomic status, and so on.
It's crucial to challenge and dismantle these systems of oppression,
To create a more just and equitable society, where shame is not used as a weapon.
Furthermore, it's essential to acknowledge that shame can be debilitating
And lead to severe mental health issues, such as depression and anxiety,
Thus it's important to seek help and support when feeling overwhelmed by shame.
Shame is a complex emotion that is deeply rooted in human nature.

It can serve both positive and negative purposes,
depending on the context and how it's approached.
It's important to challenge the power dynamics that
often underlie shame, and to seek help and support when feeling overwhelmed by
it.
Ultimately, it's through self-reflection, forgiveness,
and balance that we can learn to embrace shame as a teacher, and not let it
control us.
Moreover, it's important to remember that shame
is not always bad, and it can be used to regulate our behavior,
in order to avoid harm to ourselves or others.
But, when it becomes excessive, it can lead to
self-destructive behaviors and a lack of self-compassion.
Therefore, it's essential to develop a healthy relationship
with shame by learning to recognize it, understand its origins,
and identify the underlying thoughts and beliefs that feed it.
One of the ways to overcome shame is through self-compassion,
which is the ability to be kind, understanding and supportive towards oneself,
especially in moments of failure or inadequacy.
It's about treating oneself with the same kindness, concern,
and forgiveness as one would offer to a good friend.
Another way to overcome shame is through self-forgiveness,
which is the ability to give oneself permission to make mistakes, l
earn from them, and move on.
In addition, it's important to surround oneself with supportive
and understanding people, who can help in the process of healing and growth.
Finally, it's essential to remember that shame is not a permanent state,
and that we all have the power to change and grow.
In conclusion, shame is a complex emotion that can have both positive
and negative effects on our lives.
It's important to develop a healthy relationship with it by recognizing it,

understanding its origins, and learning to practice self-compassion, self-forgiveness, and surround ourselves with supportive people. It's through these practices that we can learn to embrace shame as a teacher, and not let it control us.

6. Culturally Constructed Virginity

Veracity of virginity, a concept oft-discussed,
A metaphor for life, in which it is thus cussed,
A state of being, pure and untouched,
Yet oft-misunderstood, and oft-maligned as such.

But what is this thing, that we call virginity,
Is it a physical state, or an ethereal entity?
A hymen, unbroken, or a mind, unsullied,
Or is it a societal construct, that's been glorified?

The term "virginity" is a social construct.
It's a set of beliefs and expectations that society has erected.
It's not a physical state, but rather a cultural one,
that's been used to control and regulate.

The concept of virginity is a metaphor for life,
It represents the idea that one can only live once,
One can only experience life in a certain way,
One can only be a certain kind of person.

It is a metaphor for the idea that we are all unique,
That we all have our own path to follow,
That we all have something special to offer,
And that we should be proud of that uniqueness.

But let us not forget, that virginity is but a state,
A fleeting moment in the grand scheme of fate,
For life is ever-changing, and so are we,
And to truly live, one must be set free.

So let us break free from the shackles of virginity,
And embrace the beauty of diversity,
For life is not a one-time event,
But a journey, with no end.

And as we journey through this thing called life,
We must not be bound by societal strife,
For virginity is but a small part of the whole,
And to truly live, one must let go of control.

We must embrace the unknown, and take risks,
For it is through these that true growth exists,
For life is not a destination, but a journey,
And it's through experiences that we truly learn.

So let us not be defined by our virginity,
But rather by the choices we make and the paths we see,
For in the grand scheme of things, it matters not,
But how we live our lives, that is what we've got.

For life is a metaphor for virginity,
A journey to be lived, a story to be written,
And as we navigate through its twists and turns,
Let us remember that our worth is not in what we've earned.

So let us live our lives with passion and grace,
And let go of societal constructs that hold us in place,
For in the end, it is not virginity that defines us,
But the way we live our lives, and the love that surrounds us.

And as we journey through this thing called life,
We must not be bound by societal strife,
For virginity is but a small part of the whole,
And to truly live, one must let go of control.

We must embrace the unknown, and take risks,
For it is through these that true growth exists,
For life is not a destination, but a journey,
And it's through experiences that we truly learn.

So let us not be defined by our virginity,
But rather by the choices we make and the paths we see,
For in the grand scheme of things, it matters not,
But how we live our lives, that is what we've got.

For life is a metaphor for virginity,
A journey to be lived, a story to be written,
And as we navigate through its twists and turns,
Let us remember that our worth is not in what we've earned.

So let us live our lives with passion and grace,
And let go of societal constructs that hold us in place,
For in the end, it is not virginity that defines us,
But the way we live our lives, and the love that surrounds us.

And as we reach the end of our journey,

And look back on the path we've traversed,
Let us not regret the choices we've made,
But cherish the memories and lessons we've earned.

For life is a precious gift, a metaphor for virginity,
A journey to be savored, a story to be shared,
And as we look to the horizon,
Let us embrace the future, unafraid.

And as we journey on through life,
Let us not be constrained by societal strife,
For virginity is but a small part of the whole,
And to truly live, we must let go of control.

We must not be defined by societal norms,
But rather, by the choices we make, and the paths we form,
For life is a canvas, and we are the artists,
And it's through our experiences, that our true selves are the brightest.

So let us not let virginity, or lack thereof,
Define who we are, or limit our growth,
For life is a journey, and we are free souls,
And our worth is not determined by societal roles.

For life is a metaphor for virginity,
A journey to be embraced, a story to be told,
And as we journey on, let us not look back,
But cherish the memories, and the love that we hold.

For in the end, it is not virginity,
But the way we lived our lives, that will set us free,

And in the grand scheme of things, it matters not,
But the love we shared, and the memories we've got.

And so let us not be defined by our virginity,
But by the love and experiences we've accumulated,
For life is not a singular state,
But a journey of growth and self-creation.

Let us not be constrained by societal constructs,
But rather, let us live our lives with open hearts,
For virginity is but a small part of the grand scheme,
And true living comes from embracing one's true dream.

And as we journey through this thing called life,
Let us not be limited by fear or societal strife,
For true living comes from taking risks,
And embracing the unknown, with a sense of vitality.

For life is a metaphor for virginity,
A journey to be explored, a story to be told,
And as we navigate through its twists and turns,
Let us remember that our worth is not in what we hold.

So let us live our lives with passion and grace,
And let go of societal expectations, that hold us in place,
For in the end, it is not virginity that defines us,
But the way we live our lives, and the love that surrounds us.

And as we journey through this thing called life,
Let us not be held back by societal strife,
For virginity is but a small part of the grand scheme,

And true living comes from embracing our true theme.

We must not be defined by societal norms,
But by the choices we make, and the paths we form,
For life is a canvas, and we are the artists,
And it's through our experiences, that our true selves are the brightest.

Let us not let virginity, or lack thereof,
Be a source of shame or guilt, but rather a cause for growth,
For life is a journey, and we are free souls,
And our worth is not determined by societal roles.

For life is a metaphor for virginity,
A journey to be embraced, a story to be told,
And as we journey on, let us not look back,
But cherish the memories, and the love that we hold.

So let us break free from the shackles of virginity,
And embrace the beauty of diversity,
For life is not a one-time event,
But a journey, with no end.

As we continue on our journey through life,
Let us not be constrained by societal expectations,
For virginity, in the grand scheme of things,
Is but a small part of our true existence.

Let us not be defined by our sexual experiences,
But by the love and connections we've created,
For true living comes from embracing one's true self,
And living authentically, unafraid and un-hated.

And let us not forget, that virginity is not a prize,
To be won or lost, but rather a state of mind,
For true purity and innocence, lies within the soul,
And it's a journey that one can always find.

So let us not judge, or be judged by virginity,
But rather, let us embrace the beauty of diversity,
For life is a journey, with no end in sight,
And it's through our experiences, that we truly thrive.

As we journey through this thing called life,
Let us not be held back by societal expectations,
For virginity is but a small part of the grand scheme,
And true living comes from embracing our true dream.

We must not be defined by societal norms,
But by the choices we make, and the paths we form,
For life is a canvas, and we are the artists,
And it's through our experiences, that our true selves are the brightest.

So let us not let virginity, or lack thereof,
Be a source of shame or guilt, but rather a cause for growth,
For life is a journey, and we are free souls,
And our worth is not determined by societal roles.

For life is a metaphor for virginity,
A journey to be embraced, a story to be told,
And as we journey on, let us not look back,
But cherish the memories, and the love that we hold.

Let us not be limited by societal constructs,
But rather, let us live our lives with open hearts,
For virginity is but a small part of the grand scheme,
And true living comes from embracing one's true dream.

As we journey through this thing called life,
Let us not be held back by societal expectations and constructs,
For virginity is but a small part of the grand scheme,
And true living comes from embracing our own unique theme.

We must not be defined by societal norms and stereotypes,
But by the choices we make, and the paths we explore,
For life is a canvas, and we are the artists,
And it's through our experiences, that our true selves are revealed more.

So let us not let virginity, or lack thereof,
Be a source of shame or guilt, but rather an opportunity for growth,
For life is a journey, and we are free souls,
And our worth is not determined by societal roles.

For life is a metaphor for virginity,
A journey to be embraced, a story to be told,
And as we journey on, let us not look back,
But cherish the memories, and the love that we hold.

Let us not be limited by societal constructs,
But rather, let us live our lives with open hearts,
For virginity is but a small part of the grand scheme,
And true living comes from embracing our unique theme.

As we journey through this thing called life,

Let us not be constrained by societal expectations and constructs,
For virginity is but a small part of the grand scheme,
And true living comes from embracing our own unique dream.

Let us not be defined by societal norms and stereotypes,
But by the choices we make and the paths we explore,
For life is a canvas, and we are the artists,
And it's through our experiences that our true selves are revealed more.

So let us not let virginity, or lack thereof,
Be a source of shame or guilt, but rather a chance for growth,
For life is a journey, and we are free souls,
And our worth is not determined by societal roles.

For life is a metaphor for virginity,
A journey to be embraced, a story to be told,
And as we journey on, let us not look back,
But cherish the memories and the love that we hold.

Let us not be limited by societal constructs,
But rather, let us live our lives with open hearts,
For virginity is but a small part of the grand scheme,
And true living comes from embracing our unique dream.

7. Creativitas Exploration

In the realm of thought and imagination,
Where ideas and concepts germinate and bloom,
Lies the essence of creativity,
A force that drives the human mind to innovate and consume.

It is a power that defies all explanation,
A mystery that science struggles to decode,
A spark that ignites the mind's passion,
A fire that burns with an unquenchable load.

But what is creativity, truly?
Is it the ability to create something new,
Or is it the capacity to see things differently,
To view the world in a hue?

Perhaps it is a combination of both,
A fusion of innovation and perception,
A synergy of mind and soul,
A reflection of the human connection.

For creativity is not just a product,
But a process, a journey of exploration,
A quest to discover and uncover,
The depths of the human imagination.

It is the ability to transcend the mundane,

To break free from the constraints of reality,
To soar beyond the limits of the ordinary,
And create something truly spectacularly.

But creativity is not just for the artist,
It is for all who seek to innovate,
It is for the scientist, the engineer,
For those who seek to create and elevate.

For creativity is the driving force,
Of progress and evolution,
It is the source of our greatest achievements,
And the key to our ultimate solution.

So let us embrace our creativity,
And let it guide us on our way,
For in its boundless power and potential,
Lies the path to a brighter tomorrow, today.

But creativity is not always easy,
It requires hard work and dedication,
It demands that we push ourselves,
To confront our fears and limitations.

For creativity is a double-edged sword,
It can bring both joy and pain,
It can inspire us to greatness,
Or drive us to madness and disdain.

But it is through this struggle,
That we truly discover our selves,

For it is in the act of creating,
That we find meaning and purpose,

Creativity is not just about making,
It's about understanding,
It's about seeing the world,
And ourselves, in a different light.

It's about taking risks,
And embracing the unknown,
It's about accepting the failures,
And learning from them, to grow.

For creativity is not a destination,
But a journey, an ongoing quest,
It is a path of self-discovery,
And a way to find inner rest.

So let us embrace our creativity,
And let it guide us on our way,
For in its boundless power and potential,
Lies the path to a brighter tomorrow, today.

Let us not be afraid to create,
To explore the depths of our mind,
For in the act of creating,
We will find the answers we seek to find.

For creativity is the force that drives us,
The spark that ignites our soul,
It is the key to our evolution,

And the reason for our ultimate goal.

So let us honor the creative spirit,
And let it guide us on our way,
For in its boundless power and potential,
Lies the path to a brighter tomorrow, today.

But let us not forget,
That creativity is not just for the individual,
It is for the collective as well,
For the betterment of the entire community.

For when we come together,
In the spirit of creativity and collaboration,
We can achieve something greater,
Than what we could have ever achieved alone.

Creativity knows no bounds,
And it knows no limits,
It is a force that unites us all,
And it helps us to achieve our shared objectives.

So let us strive to foster creativity,
In ourselves, and in others around us,
For in doing so, we will build a better future,
And a more inclusive, and harmonious society.

For creativity is not just about making art,
It is about making the world a better place,
It is about finding solutions,
And making a difference in the human race.

So let us embrace our creativity,
And let it guide us on our way,
For in its boundless power and potential,
Lies the path to a brighter tomorrow, today.

Let us not be afraid to create,
To explore the depths of our mind,
For in the act of creating,
We will find the answers we seek to find.

For creativity is the force that drives us,
The spark that ignites our soul,
It is the key to our evolution,
And the reason for our ultimate goal.

So let us honor the creative spirit,
And let it guide us on our way,
For in its boundless power and potential,
Lies the path to a brighter tomorrow, today.

But let us not forget,
That creativity is not only about making,
It is also about questioning,
And challenging what we know to be true.

For creativity is not just about the present,
But also about the future,
It is about shaping and molding,
The world that we want to see.

It is about taking risks,
And stepping outside of our comfort zone,
It is about pushing boundaries,
And making a difference on our own.

For creativity is not just about what we make,
But about how we think and feel,
It is about how we approach the world,
And how we make our mark on the deal.

So let us embrace our creativity,
And let it guide us on our way,
For in its boundless power and potential,
Lies the path to a brighter tomorrow, today.

Let us not be afraid to create,
To explore the depths of our mind,
For in the act of creating,
We will find the answers we seek to find.

For creativity is the force that drives us,
The spark that ignites our soul,
It is the key to our evolution,
And the reason for our ultimate goal.

So let us honor the creative spirit,
And let it guide us on our way,
For in its boundless power and potential,
Lies the path to a brighter tomorrow, today. Let us embrace our creativity,
For it is the key to our progress and evolution,
It is the engine that drives us,

And the light that guides us on our path to resolution.

So let us embrace our creativity,
And let it flow freely and wild,
Let us not be afraid to experiment,
And let our imaginations run wild.

For creativity is not just about perfection,
But about exploration and experimentation,
It is about taking risks,
And pushing the boundaries of our imagination.

For creativity is not just about the end result,
But about the journey, the process,
It is about the struggles and the triumphs,
And how they shape us and impress.

So let us embrace our creativity,
And let it guide us on our way,
For in its boundless power and potential,
Lies the path to a brighter tomorrow, today.

Let us not be afraid to create,
To explore the depths of our mind,
For in the act of creating,
We will find the answers we seek to find.

For creativity is the force that drives us,
The spark that ignites our soul,
It is the key to our evolution,
And the reason for our ultimate goal.

So let us honor the creative spirit,
And let it guide us on our way,
For in its boundless power and potential,
Lies the path to a brighter tomorrow, today.

Let us embrace our creativity,
For it is the key to our progress,
And the light that guides us,
On our journey to success.

But let us not forget,
That creativity is not just about the self,
It is also about the collective,
And the impact we can have on the world.

For creativity is not just about making art,
But about making a difference,
It is about finding solutions,
And making the world a better place in the instance.

So let us use our creativity,
To make a positive impact on society,
Let us not be afraid to challenge,
And make a change in the community.

For creativity is not just about personal gain,
But about creating a better world for all,
It is about using our imagination,
To make a difference big or small.

So let us embrace our creativity,
And let it guide us on our way,
For in its boundless power and potential,
Lies the path to a brighter tomorrow, today.

Let us not be afraid to create,
To explore the depths of our mind,
For in the act of creating,
We will find the answers we seek to find.

For creativity is the force that drives us,
The spark that ignites our soul,
It is the key to our evolution,
And the reason for our ultimate goal.

So let us honor the creative spirit,
And let it guide us on our way,
For in its boundless power and potential,
Lies the path to a brighter tomorrow, today.

Let us use our creativity,
For the betterment of all,
Let it be the force,
That helps us to stand tall.

But let us not forget,
That creativity is not just about the tangible,
It is also about the intangible,
And the impact it can have on our being.

For creativity is not just about making things,

But about exploring emotions,
It is about tapping into our inner selves,
And finding deeper connections.

So let us embrace our creativity,
And use it as a tool for self-discovery,
Let us not be afraid to delve into our emotions,
And find new ways to express our inner glory.

For creativity is not just about the external,
But about the internal,
It is about understanding ourselves,
And finding our own personal spin.

So let us embrace our creativity,
And let it guide us on our way,
For in its boundless power and potential,
Lies the path to a brighter tomorrow, today.

Let us not be afraid to create,
To explore the depths of our mind,
For in the act of creating,
We will find the answers we seek to find.

For creativity is the force that drives us,
The spark that ignites our soul,
It is the key to our evolution,
And the reason for our ultimate goal.

So let us honor the creative spirit,
And let it guide us on our way,

For in its boundless power and potential,
Lies the path to a brighter tomorrow, today.

Let us use our creativity,
To understand ourselves,
And to find inner peace,
In the midst of chaos and the shelves.

But let us not forget,
That creativity is not just about us,
It is also about the world around us,
And the impact we can have on the environment.

For creativity is not just about making things,
But about finding ways to sustain and preserve,
It is about using our imagination,
To create a more sustainable future.

So let us embrace our creativity,
And use it to find solutions to environmental issues,
Let us not be afraid to think outside the box,
And make a difference in the world's future.

For creativity is not just about personal gain,
But about creating a better world for all,
It is about using our imagination,
To make a difference big or small.

So let us embrace our creativity,
And let it guide us on our way,
For in its boundless power and potential,

Lies the path to a brighter tomorrow, today.

Let us not be afraid to create,
To explore the depths of our mind,
For in the act of creating,
We will find the answers we seek to find.

For creativity is the force that drives us,
The spark that ignites our soul,
It is the key to our evolution,
And the reason for our ultimate goal.

So let us honor the creative spirit,
And let it guide us on our way,
For in its boundless power and potential,
Lies the path to a brighter tomorrow, today.

Let us use our creativity,
To protect the world around us,
And to create a sustainable future,
For all of us.

Amidst the gleaming circuits and wires,
A world of technology doth transpire,
A realm of innovation and design,
Where creativity doth forever shine.

But what is this thing we call creativity,
That sparks within the mind's electricity,
Is it mere algorithms and code,
Or something more, a higher abode?

Some argue that true creativity,
Is but the product of humanity,
A gift bestowed upon us alone,
In contrast to machines of stone.

Yet others posit a different view,
That creativity is but a breakthrough,
A process of experimentation and iteration,
Available to all, without discrimination.

Whether born of man or machine,
Creativity doth forever gleam,
A beacon of progress and advancement,
In a world of technology's enhancement.

So let us embrace the creative spark,
That doth reside within the dark,
For in its light, our world doth evolve,
And with it, we too, shall evolve.

As we delve deeper into the realm of technology,
The lines between man and machine begin to blur,
For in this world of code and circuitry,
Creativity knows no bounds, no barrier.

With each passing day, machines become more adept,
At tasks once thought the sole domain of the intellect,
And yet, as we marvel at their capabilities,
We must not forget our own humanity.

For it is our humanity that gives our creations soul,
That imbues them with meaning and purpose, whole,
And as we continue to push the boundaries of what is possible,
We must remember to keep our humanity indispensable.

As we strive to create new and wondrous things,
We must not lose sight of what it means to be human beings,
For it is only by embracing both technology and humanity,
That we can truly reach our full potential, with humility.

So let us continue to explore this world of technology,
With open minds and hearts, and let our creativity be free,
For it is in the fusion of man and machine,
That we will find true progress, and a brighter future gleam.

But as we navigate this world of technology,
We must also be mindful of its darker possibility,
For with the power to create, comes the power to destroy,
And it is our responsibility to use it with joy.

For as we create new technologies,
We must consider the impact on society,
And strive to use it for the betterment of all,
Not just for the benefit of a select few.

We must also be mindful of the unintended consequences,
Of our creations and strive to mitigate their presence,
For as we continue to push the boundaries of what is possible,
We must consider the ramifications of our actions, and be responsible.

In the end, it is not about the technology itself,

But about how we choose to use it, and our wealth,
For it is not machines that shape our world,
But the choices we make, that ultimately unfurl.

So let us embrace the power of creativity,
With open minds and hearts, and a sense of responsibility,
For it is through our choices, that the world of technology,
Will become a place of wonder and prosperity.

But as we harness the power of technology,
We must also be cognizant of its propensity,
To shape not just our world, but also our very thoughts,
As we become increasingly reliant on its support.

For as we outsource our memories to the cloud,
And rely on machines to think for us aloud,
We risk losing touch with the essence of our being,
And becoming mere vessels for technology's fleeting.

We must also be wary of the power dynamics,
That come with the increasing automation of economics,
For as machines take over jobs once done by man,
We must ensure that all have a fair chance at a new plan.

As we continue to explore the depths of technology,
We must also examine the ethics and morality,
For as we shape our future with each creation,
We must ensure that it serves the greater good, with preservation.

So let us embrace the power of technology,
With a sense of caution, and responsibility,

For it is through our choices and actions,
That we shape not just our future, but also our interactions.

In this world of technology, where the future is now,
We must also consider the impact on nature, and how,
As we continue to push the boundaries of what is possible,
We must ensure that we do not harm the environment, and dispose

We must consider the long-term effects of our actions,
And strive to make technology more sustainable, with satisfaction,
By embracing renewable energy, and reducing waste,
We can ensure that technology serves as a tool, not a burden, to be faced.

We must also consider the impact of technology on privacy,
And strive to protect it, with the utmost civility,
For as we continue to digitize every aspect of our lives,
We must ensure that our personal information is safe, and thrives.

As we continue to explore the world of technology,
We must also be mindful of the impact on humanity,
For as we shape our future with each creation,
We must ensure that it serves the greater good, with preservation.

So let us embrace the power of technology,
With a sense of caution, and responsibility,
For it is through our choices and actions,
That we shape not just our future, but also our interactions.

And as we move forward in this world of technology,
We must also consider the impact on humanity's unity,
For as we become more connected, we must also be aware,

Of the potential for division, and strive to repair.

With the rise of social media and the internet,
We have access to more information than ever, but we mustn't forget,
That with this access comes the potential for manipulation,
And we must strive to seek out truth, and not fall for fabrication.

We must also consider the impact of technology on culture,
And strive to preserve the diversity, that is the world's feature,
For as we continue to push the boundaries of what is possible,
We must ensure that we do not homogenize, and lose the unique, accountable.

As we continue to explore the world of technology,
We must also examine the ethics and morality,
For as we shape our future with each creation,
We must ensure that it serves the greater good, with preservation.

So let us embrace the power of technology,
With a sense of caution, and responsibility,
For it is through our choices and actions,
That we shape not just our future, but also our interactions.

And as we continue to advance in this world of technology,
We must also consider the impact on humanity's mental health, and its ecology,
For as we become more reliant on screens and digital devices,
We must be mindful of the potential for addiction and negative consequences.

We must also consider the impact of technology on our physical health,
And strive to find balance, and not let technology control our wealth,
For as we continue to push the boundaries of what is possible,
We must ensure that we do not neglect our well-being and health, accountable.

As we continue to explore the world of technology,
We must also examine the ethics and morality,
For as we shape our future with each creation,
We must ensure that it serves the greater good, with preservation.

So let us embrace the power of technology,
With a sense of caution, and responsibility,
For it is through our choices and actions,
That we shape not just our future, but also our interactions.

As the world of technology continues to expand,
We must remember that it is ultimately in our hands,
To use it for the betterment of all, not just a select few,
And strive to find balance, and not let technology control us.

8. The Grass' Winter Hymn

Upon the barren plain where once lush blades did sway,
A parched and withered field doth now display.
The winter winds doth blow with bitter breath,
Upon the dry grass, a symbol of life's test.

For as the grass doth wilt and fade away,
So too do we, in time, to dust decay.
But in the bleak and barren winter's grasp,
A glimmer of hope doth still securely clasp.

For though the grass doth seem to fade and die,
It sleeps beneath the snow, to rise anew by and by.
And so it is with life, in every stage,
For death doth not the end, but merely turn the page.

For every winter, there doth spring arise,
Bringing with it new growth, new life, new skies.
And so we too, shall rise from death's embrace,
To live anew, in a higher, brighter place.

The dry grass in the winter is but a metaphor,
Of life's eternal cycle, forever more.
So let us not despair in life's dark hour,
For spring doth always follow winter's shower.

And as we walk upon the dry grass,

We must remember, nothing does truly pass.
For even in the depths of winter's cold,
Life persists, in forms both young and old.

The seeds that sleep beneath the barren ground,
Will soon enough, by spring's warmth be found.
And so it is with us, in our darkest days,
A seed of life within us, never truly fades.

For as the dry grass in winter doth attest,
Life is a cycle, forever in its quest.
To rise and fall, to bloom and fade,
But always to return, in nature's grand parade.

So let us take heart, and let us be bold,
For life doth always find a way to unfold.
The dry grass in winter is but a sign,
Of the eternal dance of life, forever entwined.

So let us tread upon the dry grass with grace,
And trust in the cycle of life, in its ever-changing pace.
For though we may wilt and fade, just like the grass,
We too shall rise again, in nature's eternal mass.

As we gaze upon the dry grass in winter's hold,
We must remember, it is not a story told.
It is a reminder, that life is not forever,
But in its transience, true beauty we discover.

For it is in the dry grass, we see the beauty of change,
The way life ebbs and flows, in an endless range.

And as the dry grass withers, it makes way for the new,
A reminder that life is constantly renew.

So let us not cling to the past, or fear the unknown,
For in the dry grass, we see that life goes on.
And as the winter's chill doth ravage the land,
We must trust that spring will soon take its hand.

For the dry grass in winter, is not the end,
But a step in the journey, a chapter to befriend.
It teaches us that life is not permanent,
But the journey and the experience is what's relevant.

So let us walk upon the dry grass in winter's light,
With open hearts and minds, ready for what's in sight.
For in the dry grass, we see the beauty of life,
A metaphor for our own journey, free from strife.

As we tread upon the dry grass in the winter's cold,
Let us remember the lessons it has told.
For it is in the dry grass, we see the cycle of life,
The way it ebbs and flows, without any strife.

It is a reminder, that life is not forever,
But in its transience, true beauty we discover.
As the dry grass withers and fades away,
We must trust in the cycle of life, come what may.

For just as the dry grass will rise again in spring,
So too shall we, in life's eternal ring.
For the dry grass in winter, is not the end,

But a step in the journey, a chapter to befriend.

So let us walk upon the dry grass, with open hearts and minds,
Ready for the journey, with nature's ways aligned.
For in the dry grass, we see the beauty of life,
A metaphor for our own journey, free from strife.

And as we walk upon the dry grass, in winter's cold,
Let us remember, that life is a story, yet to be told.

As we walk upon the dry grass in winter's chill,
Let us ponder the mysteries life doth still.
For the dry grass, though dormant and still,
Holds within it, the power to renew and thrill.

For just as the dry grass in winter seems to sleep,
It awakens in spring, with new growth to reap.
And so it is with us, in life's ebb and flow,
We too shall rise again, with new life to show.

The dry grass in winter, a metaphor so true,
Of the cycle of life, forever anew.
For though we may wilt and fade, just like the grass,
We too shall rise again, in nature's grand mass.

So let us walk upon the dry grass, with eyes aglow,
And in its beauty, the secrets of life we'll know.
For in the dry grass, we see the cycle of life,
A reminder that in death, new beginnings are rife.

So let us walk upon the dry grass, with wonder and awe,

For it is in its silence, we hear nature's call.
And in the dry grass, we find hope and grace,
For in life's cycle, we see our own place.

As we tread upon the dry grass in winter's cold,
Let us not forget the stories it has told.
For in the dry grass, we see the cycle of life,
The way it ebbs and flows, without any strife.

It is a reminder that life is not forever,
But in its transience, true beauty we discover.
For in the dry grass, we see the beauty of change,
The way it makes way for new growth and new range.

So let us walk upon the dry grass, with open hearts and minds,
Ready for the journey, with nature's ways aligned.
For in the dry grass, we see the beauty of life,
A metaphor for our own journey, free from strife.

And as we walk upon the dry grass, in winter's cold,
Let us remember, that life is a story, yet to be told.
A story of growth, of change, and of rebirth,
A story that continues, from our time of birth.

So let us walk upon the dry grass, with hope and grace,
For in its withered form, we see life's eternal face.
For the dry grass in winter, is not the end,
But a step in the journey, a chapter to befriend.

As we walk upon the dry grass in winter's cold,
Let us take a moment, to behold.

For the dry grass, though dormant and still,
Holds within it, the power to renew and thrill.

For in the dry grass, we see the cycle of life,
The way it ebbs and flows, without any strife.
And as the dry grass withers and fades away,
We must trust in the cycle of life, come what may.

For just as the dry grass will rise again in spring,
So too shall we, in life's eternal ring.
And as we walk upon the dry grass, we see the beauty of death,
For it is the end of one cycle and the start of another, with nothing left.

The dry grass in winter, a reminder of the impermanence of all things,
A metaphor for the fleeting nature of life's fleeting wings.
So let us walk upon the dry grass, with humility and grace,
For in its withered form, we see the fleeting nature of time and space.

And as we walk upon the dry grass, let us embrace,
The beauty and the mystery of life's ever-changing pace.
For in the dry grass, we see the cycle of birth, death, and rebirth,
A reminder that life is a journey, forever worth.

As we walk upon the dry grass in winter's cold,
Let us remember the stories it has told.
For the dry grass, though dormant and still,
Holds within it, the power to renew and thrill.

For in the dry grass, we see the cycle of life,
The way it ebbs and flows, without any strife.
And as the dry grass withers and fades away,

We must trust in the cycle of life, come what may.

For just as the dry grass will rise again in spring,
So too shall we, in life's eternal ring.
And as we walk upon the dry grass, we see the beauty of death,
For it is the end of one cycle and the start of another, nothing left.

The dry grass in winter, a reminder of the impermanence of all things,
A metaphor for the fleeting nature of life's fleeting wings.
So let us walk upon the dry grass, with humility and grace,
For in its withered form, we see the fleeting nature of time and space.

And as we walk upon the dry grass, let us embrace
The beauty and the mystery of life's ever-changing pace.
For in the dry grass, we see the cycle of life and death,
A reminder that in the end, nothing is left.

So let us walk upon the dry grass, with open hearts and minds,
Ready for the journey, with nature's ways aligned.
For in the dry grass, we see the beauty of life,
A metaphor for our own journey, free from strife.

9. Whispers of Insight: An Exploration of Intuition

In the realm of thought, where reason reigns supreme,
A subtle force doth quietly scheme,
Intuition, 'tis called, a force quite unclear,
But one that guides us, 'ere we know it's here.

It whispers in our ears, a silent plea,
Guiding us to truths we cannot see,
A sixth sense, if you will, a gut reaction,
A spark of insight, born of pure intuition.

But what is intuition, truly so,
A fickle muse, or guiding glow?
Science doth seek to understand,
But answers, thus far, are hard to land.

Some say 'tis a product of the brain,
A culmination of life's experiences and strains,
Others claim 'tis a spiritual force,
A connection to a higher source.

Perhaps 'tis a combination of both,
A bridge between the tangible and cloth,
A meeting point of science and belief,
A subtle force that brings us relief.

But whether 'tis nature or divine,
Intuition doth remain a sign,
Of the complexity of the human mind,
And the depth of knowledge yet to find.

So let us heed the call of intuition,
For it doth bring a sense of resolution,
And though it may be hard to define,
It is a force that doth align.

And so we must delve deeper still,
To unlock the secrets of intuition's thrill,
For though it may seem fleeting and ephemeral,
It is a force that doth shape us, infernal.

Intuition doth shape our every move,
Guiding us in matters of love and groove,
It doth lead us to our passions true,
And helps us navigate the world anew.

But like all things, intuition doth have its flaw,
For sometimes it doth lead us to a moral claw,
And so we must learn to trust, but also verify,
To balance intuition's pull, with reason's eye.

And so we must strive to understand,
Intuition's role in this great cosmic band,
For it is a force that doth shape our fate,
And holds the key to a brighter state.

So let us embrace intuition's call,
And heed its voice, one and all,
For it is a force that doth guide us true,
And holds the power to make our dreams come true.

But as we delve deeper still,
And seek to understand intuition's thrill,
We must also acknowledge its limits,
For intuition is not always the wisest of wits.

It is not infallible, nor free of bias,
And so we must be mindful of its basis,
And use it as a tool, not a crutch,
To guide us forward, not hold us in a hutch.

For intuition, like all things, must evolve,
To better serve and better resolve,
And so we must seek to educate,
And to refine our intuition's state.

And so let us use intuition as a guide,
But always keep our reason by our side,
For together they can lead us to great heights,
And unlock the secrets of the universe's delights.

Intuition, a force both subtle and grand,
A mystery yet to be fully understood, but oh so grand,
As we continue to explore its depths and bounds,
We shall uncover its secrets, and its profound profound.

For intuition is a part of our humanity,

A reflection of our mind's complexity,
It is a gift, to be treasured and revered,
But also a challenge, that must be cleared.

So let us embrace intuition's call,
And heed its voice, one and all,
For it is a force that doth guide us true,
And holds the power to make our dreams come true.

But let us also strive to understand,
The nuances and subtleties of intuition's brand,
For as we do, we shall unlock its true potential,
And unlock the secrets of our own essential.

And as we continue on this journey,
To explore the depths of intuition's story,
We must not forget to listen to our heart,
For it is there where intuition's spark doth start.

For intuition is not just a thing of the mind,
But a connection to the body and the heart entwined,
It is a balance between logic and emotion,
A harmonious fusion, in perfect motion.

And so let us learn to trust our intuition,
But also to question and to make a resolution,
For intuition is not a magic solution,
But a tool to be used with discretion and caution.

So let us embrace intuition's call,
And heed its voice, one and all,

For it is a force that doth guide us true,
And holds the power to make our dreams come true.

As we continue to unravel the mysteries of intuition,
We can gain a greater understanding of our own nature and the world's fusion.

And with this understanding, we can use intuition
As a guide to navigate through life's mission,
To make better choices and to live more fully,
And to find true purpose and meaning, wholly.

For intuition is not just a thing of the past,
But a force that doth shape our future's cast,
It is a key to unlock our potential,
And to reach for greatness, essential.

So let us embrace intuition's call,
And heed its voice, one and all,
For it is a force that doth guide us true,
And holds the power to make our dreams come true.

And as we continue on this journey,
To explore the depths of intuition's story,
We can trust that it will lead us to a brighter future,
A path of growth, of knowledge, and of nurture.

And so, as we come to an end of this epic tale,
Of intuition and its subtle, yet powerful trail,
Let us remember to trust in our intuition,
But also to question and seek resolution.

For intuition is not a thing to be feared,
But a force to be revered,
It is a guide to navigate through life,
And to find our true purpose, without strife.

Let us embrace intuition's call,
And heed its voice, one and all,
For it is a force that doth guide us true,
And holds the power to make our dreams come true.

And as we continue on this journey,
Of self-discovery and inner-learning,
Let us remember to always trust our intuition,
For it is the compass that will always lead us to the right direction.

10. The Search for Transcendence

In the grand expanse of time and space,
A concept of the divine doth grace,
With wonder and awe, the human mind,
In search of meaning and purpose to find.

The concept of the divine, a mystery,
A subject of debate and theory,
Some argue for gods, some for none,
While others believe in the divine one.

The scientists seek the truth in facts,
In data and evidence, in logic and acts,
They find no proof of gods in the skies,
Yet, the spiritual still believe with eyes closed.

Philosophers ponder the questions deep,
Of existence and morality, of soul to keep,
They explore the nature of the divine,
And the role it plays in human design.

But perhaps the answer lies not in fact,
Or in reason, but in the heart and act,
For the divine is not a thing to find,
But a feeling, a connection of mind.

In the end, the concept of the divine,

May be but a human construct, a sign
Of our need for something greater than self,
To guide us on our journey, to help.

So let us not argue or fight,
But instead seek the divine with all our might,
For in the end, it is not the name,
But the essence, that truly remains.

And yet, the concept of the divine
Is not just a matter of faith, but also of line,
For the universe is vast, and we are but small,
And in its grandeur, we may not know it all.

Perhaps the divine is not a being,
But the energy that surrounds and brings,
Life to the galaxies, stars, and planets,
A cosmic force that never stops and grants.

The beauty of nature, the mystery of life,
The wonder of the universe, free from strife,
All speak to something greater than us,
A divine essence, that fills us with trust.

And as we ponder and reflect,
On the concept of the divine, we can't neglect,
That the search for meaning and purpose,
Is a journey for all, without any sort of closure.

For the divine is not an end, but a path,
A way to understand, to love, and to have,

A connection to something greater than our selves,
A way to transcend, and to reach a higher shelves.

So let us embrace the divine,
With open hearts and open minds,
And let it guide us on our journey,
Towards a greater understanding and harmony.

But as we seek the divine, we must remember,
That the concept is not without its splendor,
For the divine is not only a force of good,
But also of darkness, as we have understood.

The concept of the divine is not fixed,
But rather a reflection of our own mix,
Of desires, fears, and beliefs,
That shape our understanding and reliefs.

And thus, the divine can also be used,
As a tool for control, or to be abused,
By those in power, who seek to impose,
Their own beliefs, on the masses, and to impose.

So as we search for the divine, we must be aware,
Of the dangers of blind faith, and the pitfalls to ensnare,
For the divine is not only a source of light,
But also of darkness, and we must choose the right.

The search for the divine, is not an easy quest,
It requires critical thinking, and a willingness to test,
Our beliefs, and to question, what we know,

To find the truth, and to truly grow.

But in the end, the concept of the divine,
Is a reminder, that we are part of something greater,
A cosmic connection, that fills us with wonder,
And gives our lives, meaning and thunder.

And as we contemplate the divine,
We must not forget, that it is not confined,
To one religion, or one belief,
But rather, it is a universal grief.

For all cultures, throughout history,
Have sought to understand, their place in mystery,
And have created gods, and myths, and tales,
To explain the world, and its grand scales.

But the divine is not limited by these,
For it is a concept that is beyond our ease,
It is something that transcends, and connects,
All of humanity, and its complex respects.

So let us not be divided, by our beliefs,
But rather, let us come together, and find relief,
In the concept of the divine, that unites us all,
And gives us a sense of purpose, and call.

For the divine is not just a matter of faith,
But a way to understand, our place in space,
And to find meaning, in this vast expanse,
Is the ultimate goal, of our existence.

The concept of the divine,
Is a journey, that we all must incline,
To find the truth, and to understand,
Our place in the world, and to take a stand.

And as we journey on this path divine,
We must not forget to question and refine,
Our beliefs, and to seek out new knowledge,
For the divine is not stagnant, but a college.

For as our understanding of the world expands,
So too must our concept of the divine, and its demands,
For the divine is not limited by our current perception,
But rather, it is a concept of infinite dimension.

And as we seek the divine, we must also remember,
That it is not only about the grandeur, but also about the ember,
For the divine is not only in the grand cosmic scheme,
But also in the simple things, the beauty in serene.

It is in the love we share, and the kindness we extend,
It is in the connections we make, and the bonds we befriend,
For the divine is not only in the grand and the profound,
But also in the simple, and the everyday all around.

So let us not limit our search for the divine,
To grand myths and tales, but let it also be a sign,
Of the beauty in the ordinary, and the love in the small,
For the divine is not just in the grand, but in it all.

As we contemplate the concept of the divine,
we must also remember that it is not always aligned
with our own beliefs, values and understanding,
it may be something beyond our current comprehending.

The divine may take many forms,
beyond our imagination, and often transforms
into something beyond our human grasp,
something that we can only perceive as a clasp.

The divine may be a force, a being or an energy,
it may be a mystery, that we may never fully see.
It may be something that we can never fully understand,
but it is still something that we can hold in our hand.

For the divine is not just an idea, or a belief,
but rather, it is a feeling, that gives us relief.
It is the sense of connection, and of transcendence,
that fills us with hope, and gives us a sense of existence.

So let us not be afraid, to seek the divine,
even if it may not align with our own design.
For the divine is not just about what we can see,
but also about what we can feel, and what we can be.

As we continue on this journey of the divine,
let us remember to keep an open mind, and to align,
our hearts and our souls, with the cosmic force,
that guides us through life, and gives it its source.

And as we seek the divine, we must also remember,

That it is not just about the grand and the ember,
But also about the journey, and the process,
For the divine is not a destination, but a progress.

The search for the divine is not a one-time quest,
But a lifelong journey, that requires the best
Of us, our curiosity, our openness, and our devotion,
To seek the truth, and to find our own solution.

For the divine is not a fixed concept, but a fluid one,
That adapts, and evolves, and changes, as we learn.
And as we gain new insights, and new knowledge,
We must be willing to let go, of what we once acknowledged.

So let us not cling, to old beliefs, and old ways,
But rather, let us be open, to new pathways,
For the divine is not a fixed point, but a journey,
That requires us to be open, to change, and to be free.

And as we seek the divine, let us also remember,
That it is not just about us, but also about the ember,
That connects us, to others, and to the world,
For the divine is not just about the individual, but also about the swirl.

Let us seek the divine, with open hearts and open minds,
And let it guide us, on this journey, of the cosmic grinds.

And as we seek the divine, let us also remember,
That it is not just about the grand and the ember,
But also about the mystery, and the unknown,
For the divine is not always clear, and fully shown.

The divine may be something that we may never fully grasp,
It may be a mystery, that forever will last,
It may be something that we can never fully understand,
But it is still something that we can hold in our hand.

For the divine is not just a concept, but an experience,
It is not just something that we can know, but something that we can sense.
It is the feeling of awe, and the sense of wonder,
That fills us with a sense of purpose, and of thunder.

So let us not fear the unknown, and the mystery,
But rather, let us embrace it, with curiosity.
For the divine is not just about what we can see,
But also about what we can feel, and what we can be.

As we continue on this journey of the divine,
let us remember to keep an open mind, and to be kind,
To ourselves, and to others, as we seek the truth,
For the divine is not just about us, but about the cosmic youth.

And as we seek the divine, we must also remember,
That it is not just about the grand and the ember,
But also about the connection, and the relationship,
For the divine is not just about us, but about the fellowship.

The divine may not be limited to one religion or one belief,
It may be a connection that is universal and brief,
It may be something that connects us all as one,
A cosmic force that guides us, and shines like a sun.

For the divine is not just a concept, but a connection,
A bond that unites us, and gives us a sense of affection.
It is the feeling of love, and the sense of unity,
That fills us with a sense of purpose, and of serenity.

So let us not be divided, by our beliefs and our ways,
But rather, let us come together, and find peace in the rays.
For the divine is not just about what we can see,
But also about what we can feel, and what we can be.

As we continue on this journey of the divine,
let us remember to keep an open mind, and to be kind,
To ourselves, and to others, as we seek the truth,
For the divine is not just about us, but about the cosmic youth.

And as we seek the divine, we must also remember,
That it is not just about the grand and the ember,
But also about the journey, and the process,
For the divine is not a destination, but a progress.

The search for the divine is not a one-time quest,
But a lifelong journey, that requires the best
Of us, our curiosity, our openness, and our devotion,
To seek the truth, and to find our own solution.

For the divine is not a fixed concept, but a fluid one,
That adapts, and evolves, and changes, as we learn.
And as we gain new insights, and new knowledge,
We must be willing to let go, of what we once acknowledged.

So let us not cling, to old beliefs, and old ways,

But rather, let us be open, to new pathways,
For the divine is not a fixed point, but a journey,
That requires us to be open, to change, and to be free.

And as we seek the divine, let us also remember,
That it is not just about us, but also about the ember,
That connects us, to others, and to the world,
For the divine is not just about the individual, but also about the swirl.

Let us seek the divine, with open hearts and open minds,
And let it guide us, on this journey, of the cosmic grinds.

And as we journey on this path divine,
we must strive to seek the truth, and not decline,
into dogmatism, or into blind faith,
for the divine is not a matter of belief, but a matter of grace.

For the divine is not something that can be proven,
or something that can be disproven,
it is something that we can only experience,
and something that can only be perceived in silence.

It is the sense of wonder and awe,
that fills us with a sense of purpose, and a sense of more.
It is the feeling of connection, and of transcendence,
that fills us with a sense of hope, and a sense of existence.

So let us not seek the divine, with a closed mind,
but rather, let us seek it, with an open heart and a kind,
attitude, let us seek it with curiosity, and with grace,
for the divine is not a destination, but a journey, and a race.

As we continue on this journey of the divine,
let us remember to keep an open mind, and to be kind,
to ourselves, and to others, as we seek the truth,
for the divine is not just about us, but about the cosmic youth.

And as we seek the divine, we must also remember,
that the journey is not without its challenges and its ember,
For the search for the divine, can be a difficult one,
Filled with doubts, and with fears, and with questions undone.

But we must not be discouraged, by the obstacles we face,
For the divine is not about perfection, but about the grace,
That comes from the journey, and from the process,
For the divine is not a destination, but a progress.

And as we seek the divine, we must also remember,
that the journey is not just about us, but about others, and about the ember,
That connects us, to the world, and to the greater good,
For the divine is not just about the individual, but also about the brotherhood.

And as we seek the divine, we must also remember,
that the journey is not just about the grand and the ember,
But also about the mystery, and the unknown,
For the divine is not always clear, and fully shown.

But we must not be afraid, of the unknown and the mystery,
For the divine is not just about understanding, but also about the discovery.
It is about the journey, and the process,
For the divine is not a destination, but a progress.

And as we seek the divine, we must also remember,
That it is not just about ourselves, but about others, and about the ember,
That connects us, to the world, and to the greater good,
For the divine is not just about the individual, but also about the brotherhood.

So let us seek the divine, with empathy and with love,
And let it guide us, on this journey, from above.
Let us seek the divine, with curiosity and with grace,
And let it lead us, to a greater understanding, and a better place.

In the end, the concept of the divine,
Is a reminder, that we are part of something greater,
A cosmic connection, that fills us with wonder,
And gives our lives, meaning and thunder.

11. Thriving Amidst Adversity : The Burden of Avarice

In times of financial stress, the mind doth oft reel
With worry and despair, as coin doth dwindle
And bills doth pile high, with nary a reprieve
From the constant burden of monetary woe.
But what is this stress that doth so tightly weave
Itself into the fabric of our daily toil?

Perchance 'tis but the weight of daily toil
That doth bring on this stress, as coin doth dwindle
And bills doth pile high, with nary a reprieve
From the constant burden of monetary woe.
For in truth, the mind doth oft reel
With the thought of not being able to provide

For one's self and loved ones, to not provide
For basic needs doth bring on great stress.
But is it not the daily toil
That doth bring on this financial woe,
As coin doth dwindle
And bills doth pile high, with nary a reprieve?

And yet, perchance 'tis not the toil
That doth bring on this stress, but the fear
Of not being able to provide,

As coin doth dwindle
And bills doth pile high, with nary a reprieve
From the constant burden of monetary woe.

For in truth, the mind doth oft reel
With the thought of a future devoid of reprieve
From the constant burden of financial stress,
As coin doth dwindle
And bills doth pile high, with nary a reprieve
From the daily toil that doth bring on such woe.

But is it not within our power to reprieve
Ourselves from this stress, to not let toil
And fear of not being able to provide
Consume us, as coin doth dwindle
And bills doth pile high? Perchance 'tis but a change in mindset, to not let woe
Consume us, but to find a way to thrive

In times of financial stress, to thrive
And not just survive, to find reprieve
From the constant burden of monetary woe
And the weight of daily toil.
For in truth, the mind doth oft reel
But with determination and a change in mindset, coin doth not have to dwindle
And bills doth not have to pile high, with nary a reprieve.

But alas, in times of financial stress, the mind doth oft reel
With worry and despair, as coin doth dwindle
And bills doth pile high, with nary a reprieve
From the constant burden of monetary woe.
But let us not forget the power of reprieve

And the ability to thrive, even in the midst of daily toil.
For in truth, with determination and a change in mindset, we can overcome
financial stress
And not let coin dwindle and bills pile high, with nary a reprieve.

And yet, in times of financial stress, the mind doth oft reel
With the thought of not being able to provide
For one's self and loved ones, to not provide
For basic needs doth bring on great stress.
But is it not the daily toil
That doth bring on this financial woe,
As coin doth dwindle
And bills doth pile high, with nary a reprieve?

But is it not within our power to reprieve
Ourselves from this stress, to not let toil
And fear of not being able to provide
Consume us, as coin doth dwindle
And bills doth pile high? Perchance 'tis but a change in mindset, to not let woe
Consume us, but to find a way to thrive

In times of financial stress, to thrive
And not just survive, to find reprieve
From the constant burden of monetary woe
And the weight of daily toil.
For in truth, the mind doth oft reel
But with determination and a change in mindset, coin doth not have to dwindle
And bills doth not have to pile high, with nary a reprieve.

But let us not forget that financial stress
Is not just a personal burden, but a societal ill

That doth affect us all.
Thus, let us seek reprieve
Not just for ourselves, but for all,
To ease the weight of daily toil
And bring about a more just distribution of coin
So that it doth not just dwindle
For the many, while piling high for the few.

For in truth, financial stress doth bring on woe
But with unity and a shared mindset of reprieve
We can work towards a society where toil
Is not burdened by the constant struggle to provide
And where coin doth not just dwindle
But is shared and distributed, with nary a reprieve
From the constant burden of monetary woe.

And so, in times of financial stress, let us not just reel
But take action, and strive towards reprieve
For all, to ease the weight of daily toil
And bring about a fair distribution of coin
So that it doth not just dwindle
But is shared and distributed, with nary a reprieve
From the constant burden of monetary woe.

Let us not let financial stress consume us
But instead strive towards reprieve
And a society where toil
Is not burdened by the constant struggle to provide
And where coin doth not just dwindle
But is shared and distributed, with nary a reprieve
From the constant burden of monetary woe.

For in truth, the mind doth oft reel
But with determination and a change in mindset, we can overcome financial stress
And not let coin dwindle and bills pile high, with nary a reprieve.

And so, let us not despair in times of financial stress
But instead, strive for reprieve
And a society where toil
Is not burdened by the constant struggle to provide
And where coin doth not just dwindle
But is shared and distributed, with nary a reprieve
From the constant burden of monetary woe.

For in truth, the mind doth oft reel
But with determination and a change in mindset, we can overcome financial stress
And not let coin dwindle and bills pile high, with nary a reprieve.
Let us not let financial stress consume us
But instead strive towards reprieve
And a society where toil
Is not burdened by the constant struggle to provide
And where coin doth not just dwindle
But is shared and distributed, with nary a reprieve
From the constant burden of monetary woe.

In times of financial stress, let us not reel
But instead strive towards reprieve
And a society where the burden of toil
Is not weighed down by the constant struggle to provide
And where coin doth not just dwindle
But is shared and distributed, with nary a reprieve
From the constant burden of monetary woe.

For in truth, financial stress doth bring on woe
But with determination and a change in mindset, we can strive for reprieve
And a society where the burden of toil
Is not weighed down by the constant struggle to provide
And where coin doth not just dwindle
But is shared and distributed, with nary a reprieve
From the constant burden of monetary woe.

Let us not let financial stress consume us
But instead strive towards reprieve
And a society where toil
Is not burdened by the constant struggle to provide
And where coin doth not just dwindle
But is shared and distributed, with nary a reprieve
From the constant burden of monetary woe.
For in truth, the mind doth oft reel
But with determination and a change in mindset, we can overcome financial stress
And not let coin dwindle and bills pile high, with nary a reprieve.

Thus, in times of financial stress, let us strive for reprieve
And work towards a society where toil
Is not burdened by the constant struggle to provide
And where coin doth not just dwindle
But is shared and distributed, with nary a reprieve
From the constant burden of monetary woe.
For in truth, the mind doth oft reel
But with determination and a change in mindset, we can overcome financial stress
And not let coin dwindle and bills pile high, with nary a reprieve.

And so, let us not be consumed by financial stress
But instead strive for reprieve

And a society where toil
Is not burdened by the constant struggle to provide
And where coin doth not just dwindle
But is shared and distributed, with nary a reprieve
From the constant burden of monetary woe.

For in truth, the mind doth oft reel
But with determination and a change in mindset, we can overcome financial stress
And not let coin dwindle and bills pile high, with nary a reprieve.
Let us not let financial stress consume us
But instead strive towards reprieve
And a society where toil
Is not burdened by the constant struggle to provide
And where coin doth not just dwindle
But is shared and distributed, with nary a reprieve
From the constant burden of monetary woe.

In times of financial stress, let us not reel
But instead strive towards reprieve
And a society where the burden of toil
Is not weighed down by the constant struggle to provide
And where coin doth not just dwindle
But is shared and distributed, with nary a reprieve
From the constant burden of monetary woe.

For in truth, financial stress doth bring on woe
But with determination and a change in mindset, we can strive for reprieve
And a society where the burden of toil
Is not weighed down by the constant struggle to provide
And where coin doth not just dwindle
But is shared and distributed, with nary a reprieve

From the constant burden of monetary woe.

Let us not let financial stress consume us
But instead strive towards reprieve
And a society where toil
Is not burdened by the constant struggle to provide
And where coin doth not just dwindle
But is shared and distributed, with nary a reprieve
From the constant burden of monetary woe.
For in truth, the mind doth oft reel
But with determination and a change in mindset, we can overcome financial stress
And not let coin dwindle and bills pile high, with nary a reprieve.

Thus, in times of financial stress, let us strive for reprieve
And work towards a society where toil
Is not burdened by the constant struggle to provide
And where coin doth not just dwindle
But is shared and distributed, with nary a reprieve
From the constant burden of monetary woe.
For in truth, the mind doth oft reel
But with determination and a change in mindset, we can overcome financial stress
And not let coin dwindle and bills pile high, with nary a reprieve.

Let us not be content with mere reprieve
But strive for true and lasting change
Where the burden of toil
Is not weighed down by the constant struggle to provide
And where coin doth not just dwindle
But is shared and distributed, with nary a reprieve
From the constant burden of monetary woe.
For in truth, the mind doth oft reel

But with determination and a change in mindset, we can overcome financial stress
And not let coin dwindle and bills pile high, with nary a reprieve.

And so, let us not let financial stress consume us
But instead strive for true and lasting change, for reprieve
And a society where toil
Is not burdened by the constant struggle to provide
And where coin doth not just dwindle
But is shared and distributed, with nary a reprieve
From the constant burden of monetary woe.
For in truth, the mind doth

oft reel
But with determination and a change in mindset, we can overcome financial stress
And not let coin dwindle and bills pile high, with nary a reprieve.

Let us strive for a society where wealth is not hoarded
But shared and distributed with fairness and equality, reprieve
From the constant burden of financial stress
Where toil is not burdened by the constant struggle to provide
And where coin doth not just dwindle
But is shared and distributed, with nary a reprieve
From the constant burden of monetary woe.

For in truth, financial stress doth bring on woe
But with a change in mindset and a shift in values, we can strive for reprieve
And a society where toil is not burdened by the constant struggle to provide
And where coin doth not just dwindle
But is shared and distributed, with nary a reprieve
From the constant burden of monetary woe.

Let us not be content with mere reprieve
But strive for true and lasting change
Where the burden of toil
Is not weighed down by the constant struggle to provide
And where coin doth not just dwindle
But is shared and distributed, with nary a reprieve
From the constant burden of monetary woe.
For in truth, the mind doth oft reel
But with determination and a change in mindset, we can overcome financial stress
And not let coin dwindle and bills pile high, with nary a reprieve.

And so, let us strive for a society where financial stress
Is a thing of the past, where reprieve
Is a reality and not just a fleeting thought
Where toil is not burdened by the constant struggle to provide
And where coin doth not just dwindle
But is shared and distributed, with nary a reprieve
From the constant burden of monetary woe.
For in truth, the mind doth oft reel
But with determination and a change in mindset, we can overcome financial stress
And not let coin dwindle and bills pile high, with nary a reprieve.

Let us not be consumed by financial stress
But instead strive for true and lasting change, for reprieve
And a society where toil is not burdened by the constant struggle to provide
And where coin doth not just dwindle
But is shared and distributed, with nary a reprieve
From the constant burden of monetary woe.
For in truth, the mind doth oft reel
But with determination and a change in mindset, we can overcome financial stress
And not let coin dwindle and bills pile high, with nary a reprieve.

12. The Cosmic Dance of the Grain

Oh grain of sand, so small and insignificant,
Yet in thy form, a metaphor of life's existence,
Thou art but one, amongst a vast expanse,
Yet hold within thy being, a cosmic dance.

The grains that make thee, forged in fiery stars,
Born of cosmic dust, in ancient times so far,
Thy atoms, once part of a distant sun,
Now on this earth, a journey begun.

Thy being, a reminder of the endless cycle,
Of birth, growth, and death, in nature's ritual,
From dust to dust, the cycle doth repeat,
As in life, all things must have an end, meet.

But in thy smallness, thou art not alone,
For all around, a multitude of grains have grown,
Together, a beach, a desert, a dune,
A reminder of the power of the whole, not just one.

So let us learn from thee, oh grain of sand,
That in our smallness, we too are part of a grand,
Universe, that holds within its grasp,
The secrets of life, and the mysteries of the past.

For in the end, we all must return,
To the dust from which we came, to learn,
That in life, as in death, we are but a part,
Of a cosmic dance, that will forever start.

And though our time on earth may be fleeting,
Our impact, like the grains of sand, is deceiving,
For in the grand scheme of things, we are but a speck,
Yet our actions and choices, have a ripple effect.

Like the grains that make up a dune,
We may not see the impact of our actions soon,
But over time, they shape and mold,
Creating a legacy, that will be told.

So let us strive to be like thee, oh grain of sand,
To leave behind a positive impact, in this great land,
For in the end, it is not the size that matters,
But the role we play, in the grand scheme of nature.

For like the grains of sand, we may be small,
But together, we create a beauty, for all,
So let us be mindful, in our daily lives,
To be like the grain of sand, and strive to thrive.

For in the end, we are all but a grain,
A small part of the universe, in a cosmic train,
But with our actions and choices, we can make a difference,
And leave behind a legacy, that will be our existence.

And as we journey through this mortal coil,
Let us not forget, the grains of sand, that toil,
Endlessly, in the winds of time,
A metaphor for life, that is both sublime and prime.

For like the grains of sand, we are all but fleeting,
A mere moment in the grand scheme of things, fleeting,
But in that moment, we can make a difference,
A ripple in the cosmic ocean, that will persist.

So let us strive to be like thee, oh grain of sand,
To leave behind a legacy, that will be grand,
For in the end, it is not the size that counts,
But the impact we make, on the world around us.

For like the grains of sand, we may be small,
But together, we can create a beauty, for all,
So let us be mindful, in our daily lives,
To be like the grain of sand, and strive to survive.

For in the end, we are all but a grain,
A small part of the universe, in an eternal chain,
But with our actions and choices, we can make a difference,
And leave behind a legacy, that will be our existence.

And as the sands of time continue to shift,
Let us remember the lessons of the grain, so swift,
For in its simplicity, it holds a truth,
That our time on earth, is but a youth.

Like the grains that make up a dune,

Our lives may seem insignificant, but it's not true,
For in our smallness, we hold the power,
To shape the world, in this hour.

So let us strive to be like thee, oh grain of sand,
To make a positive impact, in this great land,
For in the end, it is not the size that matters,
But the role we play, in the grand scheme of nature.

For like the grains of sand, we may be small,
But together, we create a beauty, for all,
So let us be mindful, in our daily lives,
To be like the grain of sand, and strive to thrive.

For in the end, we are all but a grain,
A small part of the universe, in a cosmic train,
But with our actions and choices, we can make a difference,
And leave behind a legacy, that will be our existence.

So let us embrace the metaphor of life,
In the humble grain of sand, so rife,
With meaning and purpose, let us strive,
To make the most of our time, and truly thrive.

And as we journey through this mortal plane,
Let us not forget the lessons of the grain,
For in its simplicity, it holds a truth,
That our time on earth, is but a youth.

For like the grains that make up a dune,
Our lives may seem insignificant, but it's not true,

For in our smallness, we hold the power,
To shape the world, in this hour.

And as the sands of time continue to flow,
Let us remember, the lessons of the grain, to know,
That though our time on earth may be brief,
Our impact, can be long-lasting, and the belief.

So let us strive to be like thee, oh grain of sand,
To make a positive impact, in this great land,
For in the end, it is not the size that matters,
But the role we play, in the grand scheme of nature.

For like the grains of sand, we may be small,
But together, we create a beauty, for all,
So let us be mindful, in our daily lives,
To be like the grain of sand, and strive to thrive.

For in the end, we are all but a grain,
A small part of the universe, in a cosmic train,
But with our actions and choices, we can make a difference,
And leave behind a legacy, that will be our existence.

So let us embrace the metaphor of life,
In the humble grain of sand, so rife,
With meaning and purpose, let us strive,
To make the most of our time, and truly thrive.

And as we walk along the beach,
Let us take a moment, to ponder and reach,
The depth of meaning, in the grains of sand,

That hold the secrets, of life's grand plan.

For though we may be but a grain,
Our actions and choices, will forever remain,
A part of the great tapestry, of life,
That is constantly woven, with every strife.

So let us strive to be like thee, oh grain of sand,
To make a positive impact, in this great land,
For in the end, it is not the size that matters,
But the role we play, in the grand scheme of nature.

For like the grains of sand, we may be small,
But together, we create a beauty, for all,
So let us be mindful, in our daily lives,
To be like the grain of sand, and strive to thrive.

For in the end, we are all but a grain,
A small part of the universe, in a cosmic train,
But with our actions and choices, we can make a difference,
And leave behind a legacy, that will be our existence.

So let us embrace the metaphor of life,
In the humble grain of sand, so rife,
With meaning and purpose, let us strive,
To make the most of our time, and truly thrive.

For as the grains of sand, we are all connected,
In a cosmic dance, that is constantly directed,
Towards a greater purpose, that we may never know,
But in our smallness, we can still make a flow.

And as we stand before the endless sea,
Let us take a moment, to contemplate and see,
The beauty of the grains of sand,
And the role they play, in the grand plan.

For though we may be small and insignificant,
Our actions and choices, are ever persistent,
In shaping the world, in ways we cannot see,
But in the grand scheme of things, they will be.

So let us strive to be like thee, oh grain of sand,
To make a positive impact, in this great land,
For in the end, it is not the size that matters,
But the role we play, in the grand scheme of nature.

For like the grains of sand, we may be small,
But together, we create a beauty, for all,
So let us be mindful, in our daily lives,
To be like the grain of sand, and strive to thrive.

For in the end, we are all but a grain,
A small part of the universe, in a cosmic train,
But with our actions and choices, we can make a difference,
And leave behind a legacy, that will be our existence.

So let us embrace the metaphor of life,
In the humble grain of sand, so rife,
With meaning and purpose, let us strive,
To make the most of our time, and truly thrive.

For as the grains of sand, we are all connected,
In a cosmic dance, that is constantly directed,
Towards a greater purpose, that we may never know,
But in our smallness, we can still make a flow.

So let us take a lesson, from the grain of sand,
And strive to make a positive impact, in this great land.

And as we gaze upon the endless sky,
Let us take a moment, to contemplate and sigh,
At the beauty of the grains of sand,
And the role they play, in the great expanse.

For though we may be small and insignificant,
Our actions and choices, are ever persistent,
In shaping the world, in ways we cannot see,
But in the grand scheme of things, they will be.

So let us strive to be like thee, oh grain of sand,
To make a positive impact, in this great land,
For in the end, it is not the size that matters,
But the role we play, in the grand scheme of nature.

For like the grains of sand, we may be small,
But together, we create a beauty, for all,
So let us be mindful, in our daily lives,
To be like the grain of sand, and strive to thrive.

For in the end, we are all but a grain,
A small part of the universe, in a cosmic train,
But with our actions and choices, we can make a difference,

And leave behind a legacy, that will be our existence.

So let us embrace the metaphor of life,
In the humble grain of sand, so rife,
With meaning and purpose, let us strive,
To make the most of our time, and truly thrive.

For as the grains of sand, we are all connected,
In a cosmic dance, that is constantly directed,
Towards a greater purpose, that we may never know,
But in our smallness, we can still make a flow.

So let us take a lesson, from the grain of sand,
And strive to make a positive impact, in this great land.

For like the grains of sand, we may be small,
But together, we can create a beauty, for all.

And as we stand before the endless horizon,
Let us take a moment, to ponder and reason,
About the significance, of the grains of sand,
And the role they play, in the grand design of the land.

For though we may be small and insignificant,
Our actions and choices, are ever persistent,
In shaping the world, in ways we cannot see,
But in the grand scheme of things, they will be.

So let us strive to be like thee, oh grain of sand,
To make a positive impact, in this great land,
For in the end, it is not the size that matters,

But the role we play, in the grand scheme of nature.

For like the grains of sand, we may be small,
But together, we create a beauty, for all,
So let us be mindful, in our daily lives,
To be like the grain of sand, and strive to thrive.

For in the end, we are all but a grain,
A small part of the universe, in a cosmic train,
But with our actions and choices, we can make a difference,
And leave behind a legacy, that will be our existence.

So let us embrace the metaphor of life,
In the humble grain of sand, so rife,
With meaning and purpose, let us strive,
To make the most of our time, and truly thrive.

For as the grains of sand, we are all connected,
In a cosmic dance, that is constantly directed,
Towards a greater purpose, that we may never know,
But in our smallness, we can still make a flow.

So let us take a lesson, from the grain of sand,
And strive to make a positive impact, in this great land.

For like the grains of sand, we may be small,
But together, we can create a beauty, for all.

So let us embrace the metaphor of life,
In the humble grain of sand, so rife,
With meaning and purpose, let us strive,

To make the most of our time, and truly thrive.

13. Ethereal Ode to Destiny

And make the most of it, you'll see,
For in the grand scheme of things,
Life is but a fleeting fling.

As we traverse this mortal plane,
We seek to understand our fate,
To find the purpose of our pain,
And make sense of this grand debate.

But destiny, it seems, is vast,
A mystery that's hard to grasp,
A concept that's both old and new,
A puzzle that we're yet to solve.

Some say it's written in the stars,
A cosmic plan that's set in bars,
Others say it's in our hands,
And we must make our own commands.

But as we search for answers true,
We must remember this adage too,
That life is but a fleeting fling,
And destiny is but a fleeting thing.

For in the grand scheme of things,
We're but a small and fleeting fling,
A mere blip in the cosmic dance,
A part of the great cosmic romance.

But though our time may be so brief,
We must make the most of it, in grief,

For in the grand scheme of things,
Life is but a fleeting fling.

So let us make our own fate,
And not wait for it to be,
For in the grand scheme of things,
We are the masters of our destiny.

But as we chart our course ahead,
We must be mindful of the path we tread,
For destiny, it seems, is not
A solitary, single thought.

It's woven in a tapestry,
Of all our choices, history,
And all the lives that we have led,
And all the things that we have said.

So let us be mindful of our steps,
And choose the path that wisdom keeps,
For in the grand scheme of things,
Our fate is but a delicate string.

We must strive to understand,
The meaning of this mortal band,
And make the most of what we've got,
Before our time on earth is sought.

For in the grand scheme of things,
We are but a fleeting fling,
A spark in the grand cosmic flame,

A part of the eternal game.

So let us make our mark,
And leave a legacy that's stark,
For in the grand scheme of things,
Our destiny is what we make it to be.

As we journey through this life,
We must seek to find the balance right,
Between the path we choose to tread
And the destiny that lies ahead.

For though we may control our fate,
The universe has its own plan, great,
And as we move towards our end,
We must learn to make amends.

With the choices that we've made,
And the paths that we have strayed,
For in the grand scheme of things,
We are but a small and fleeting fling.

So let us not despair,
But find the courage to repair,
The mistakes we've made before,
And open up a new door.

For in the grand scheme of things,
We are not just mere beings,
But part of the cosmic whole,
With a purpose to fulfill and role.

So let us embrace our destiny,
And make the most of it, you'll see,
For in the grand scheme of things,
Life is but a fleeting fling,
But also a journey worth taking.

And as we navigate this ride,
We must not let our doubts abide,
For in the grand scheme of things,
Destiny is but a song it sings.

A song that we must learn to play,
With every step along the way,
A song that's filled with notes of hope,
And moments that help us cope.

So let us not be swayed,
By the fear that we'll stray,
For in the grand scheme of things,
We are but a small and fleeting fling.

We must trust in the journey,
And not be in a hurry,
For destiny, it will unfold,
As we grow older and bold.

So let us walk with grace,
And not let our fears chase,
For in the grand scheme of things,
Destiny is but a fleeting fling.

But with each step we take,
We shape our own fate,
And create a destiny that's grand,
A journey that we'll understand.

As we journey through this life,
We must seek to find the balance right,
Between the path we choose to tread,
And the destiny that lies ahead.

For though we may control our fate,
The universe has its own plan, great,
And as we move towards our end,
We must learn to make amends.

With the choices that we've made,
And the paths that we have strayed,
For in the grand scheme of things,
We are but a small and fleeting fling.

So let us not despair,
But find the courage to repair,
The mistakes we've made before,
And open up a new door.

For in the grand scheme of things,
We are not just mere beings,
But part of the cosmic whole,
With a purpose to fulfill and role.

So let us embrace our destiny,
And make the most of it, you'll see,
For in the grand scheme of things,
Life is but a fleeting fling,
But also a journey worth taking.

So let us not be afraid,
Of the destiny that's made,
For it is a journey that we'll take,
With each step, each choice, each mistake.

And as we reach the end,
We'll look back and comprehend,
That destiny is but a part,
Of the journey of the heart.

And in that journey we'll find,
A beauty of the cosmic kind,
For every twist and every turn,
Is a lesson that we'll learn.

And as we reach the end,
We'll see that destiny was not just a trend,
But a culmination of our choices,
And the love that in our hearts encloses.

So let us not be afraid,
Of the path that's yet to be laid,
For in the grand scheme of things,
Destiny is but a fleeting fling.

But with each step we take,
We shape our own fate,
And create a destiny that's grand,
A journey that we'll understand.

For in the grand scheme of things,
We are not just mere beings,
But part of the cosmic whole,
With a purpose to fulfill and role.

So let us embrace our destiny,
And make the most of it, you'll see,
For in the grand scheme of things,
Life is but a fleeting fling,
But also a journey worth taking.

A journey that will lead us to,
The ultimate truth,
The purpose and meaning of our lives,
And the beauty that within it thrives.

And as we reach the final stage,
We'll see that life was but a page,
In the grand cosmic story,
Of the beginning and the glory.

And in that final moment,
We'll see that destiny was but a component,
Of the journey that we've been through,
A journey that was meant for you.

For in the grand scheme of things,
We are but a small and fleeting fling,
But a small part of the grand design,
A purpose that is truly divine.

So let us not be swayed,
By the fears of what's to be played,
For in the grand scheme of things,
Destiny is but a fleeting fling.

But with each step we take,
We shape our own fate,
And create a destiny that's grand,
A journey that we'll understand.

For in the grand scheme of things,
We are not just mere beings,
But part of the cosmic whole,
With a purpose to fulfill and role.

So let us embrace our destiny,
And make the most of it, you'll see,
For in the grand scheme of things,
Life is but a fleeting fling,
But also a journey worth taking.

For in the grand scheme of things,
We are but a small and fleeting fling,
But a small part of the grand design,
A purpose that is truly divine.

So let us not be swayed,
By the fears of what's to be played,
For in the grand scheme of things,
Destiny is but a fleeting fling.

But with each step we take,
We shape our own fate,
And create a destiny that's grand,
A journey that we'll understand.

For in the grand scheme of things,
We are not just mere beings,
But part of the cosmic whole,
With a purpose to fulfill and role.

So let us embrace our destiny,
And make the most of it, you'll see,
For in the grand scheme of things,
Life is but a fleeting fling,
But also a journey worth taking.

A journey that will lead us to,
The ultimate truth,
The purpose and meaning of our lives,
And the beauty that within it thrives.

So let us not be afraid,
Of the destiny that's yet to be made,
For it is a journey that we'll take,
With each step, each choice, each mistake.

And as we reach the end,
We'll see that destiny was not just a trend,
But a culmination of our choices,
And the love that in our hearts encloses.

So let us embrace our destiny,
And make the most of it, you'll see,
For in the grand scheme of things,
Life is but a fleeting fling,
But also a journey worth taking.

And as we reach the end,
We'll realize that destiny was not a bend,
But a path that we have chosen,
With every step, every word spoken.

For destiny is not set in stone,
It's a journey that we must own,
A journey that's filled with choices,
And the voice of our own voices.

So let us not be swayed,
By the fears of what's to be played,
For in the grand scheme of things,
Destiny is but a fleeting fling.

But with each step we take,
We shape our own fate,
And create a destiny that's grand,
A journey that we'll understand.

For in the grand scheme of things,
We are not just mere beings,
But part of the cosmic whole,
With a purpose to fulfill and role.

So let us embrace our destiny,
And make the most of it, you'll see,
For in the grand scheme of things,
Life is but a fleeting fling,
But also a journey worth taking.

A journey that will lead us to,
The ultimate truth,
The purpose and meaning of our lives,
And the beauty that within it thrives.

So let us not be afraid,
Of the destiny that's yet to be made,
For it is a journey that we'll take,
With each step, each choice, each mistake.

And as we reach the end,
We'll see that destiny was not just a trend,
But a culmination of our choices,
And the love that in our hearts encloses.

And as we reach the end,
We'll see that destiny was not just a trend,
But a culmination of our choices,
And the love that in our hearts encloses.

So let us not be afraid,
Of the destiny that's yet to be made,
For it is a journey that we'll take,
With each step, each choice, each mistake.

For in the grand scheme of things,
Destiny is not just a string,
But a tapestry of our actions,
And the reactions of the cosmic factions.

And as we reach the end,
We'll see that destiny was not just a friend,
But a companion on our journey,
A guide that helped us find our glory.

So let us embrace our destiny,
And make the most of it, you'll see,
For in the grand scheme of things,
Life is but a fleeting fling,
But also a journey worth taking.

A journey that will lead us to,
The ultimate truth,
The purpose and meaning of our lives,
And the beauty that within it thrives.

So let us not be afraid,
Of the destiny that's yet to be made,
For it is a journey that we'll take,
With each step, each choice, each mistake.

And as we reach the end,
We'll see that destiny was not just a trend,
But a culmination of our choices,
And the love that in our hearts encloses.

For in the grand scheme of things,
Destiny is but a fleeting fling,
But a journey worth taking,
With each step, each choice, each making.

And as we reach the end,
We'll see that destiny was not just a bend,
But a path that we have chosen,
With every step, every word spoken.

For destiny is not set in stone,
It's a journey that we must own,
A journey that's filled with choices,
And the voice of our own voices.

So let us not be swayed,
By the fears of what's to be played,
For in the grand scheme of things,
Destiny is but a fleeting fling.

But with each step we take,
We shape our own fate,
And create a destiny that's grand,
A journey that we'll understand.

For in the grand scheme of things,

We are not just mere beings,
But part of the cosmic whole,
With a purpose to fulfill and role.

So let us embrace our destiny,
And make the most of it, you'll see,
For in the grand scheme of things,
Life is but a fleeting fling,
But also a journey worth taking.

A journey that will lead us to,
The ultimate truth,
The purpose and meaning of our lives,
And the beauty that within it thrives.

So let us not be afraid,
Of the destiny that's yet to be made,
For it is a journey that we'll take,
With each step, each choice, each mistake.

And as we reach the end,
We'll see that destiny was not just a trend,
But a culmination of our choices,
And the love that in our hearts encloses.

For in the grand scheme of things,
Destiny is but a fleeting fling,
But a journey worth taking,
With each step, each choice, each making.

So let us embrace our destiny,

And make the most of it, you'll see,
For in the grand scheme of things,
Life is but a fleeting fling,
But also a journey worth living.

14. The Creative Conundrum

In the depths of the human mind, there lies a curse,
A burden upon the soul, a weight without verse.
It is the call of creativity, the muses' sweet song,
That leads us down a path where freedom is forever gone.

For with each brushstroke, each note, each word we pen,
We bind ourselves in chains, our fate to the work we begin.
We pour our hearts and souls into the creations we make,
And in the process, our own selves, we forsake.

The artist, the writer, the musician, all the same,
Trapped by their own talents, in an endless, self-made chain.
They sacrifice their freedom for the sake of their art,
And in the end, they find they've given up their heart.

For the creative mind can never be at rest,
It craves new inspiration, a new challenge, a new quest.
And so the cycle continues, a never-ending spiral,
Until the artist's freedom is nothing more than a denial.

Thus, we must recognize this curse of creativity,
And understand that freedom comes at a great cost, a great penalty.
For though the muses' call may be sweet and alluring,
It is a siren's song that leads us to our own undoing.

But still, the call persists, and we cannot help but heed,

For the love of creation is a force that cannot be freed.
We cannot escape the pull, the need to create,
To bring beauty and expression to the world and our fate.

But as we succumb to the call, and our freedom we lose,
We must remember that the price of art is not for us to choose.
For though we may be trapped, and our freedom may be gone,
Our creations will live on, and in them, our legacy will spawn.

And so, we must find solace in the knowledge that our art,
Will outlive us all, and leave a mark upon the heart.
For though we may lose ourselves in the pursuit of creativity,
Our art will always be a reminder of our humanity.

So let us embrace the curse, and let our muses guide,
For in the end, it is through art that our souls will reside.
And though our freedom may be lost, our creativity will be found,
For it is in the creation of art that true freedom can be found.

But let us also remember, that in this never-ending cycle,
We must find a balance, a way to reconcile.
To nurture our creativity, while also cherishing our freedom,
To find a way to create without losing our own being.

Perhaps it is in the understanding of this paradox,
That true freedom and creativity can coexist.
For as we strive to create, let us also strive to be true,
To ourselves, our values, and our own autonomy.

Let us not be trapped by the illusions of fame and success,
But rather, let us create for the sake of our own happiness.

For it is in this way, that we can truly be free,
To create without sacrifice, and live authentically.

So let us embrace the call of creativity,
But let us also remember our own humanity.
For it is in the balance of these two opposing forces,
That we can truly find meaning and purpose in our artistic courses.

And in this way, we can truly be free,
To create without sacrifice, and live authentically.

Let us also remember that our creations are not just for ourselves,
But for the world, to be shared and experienced by others.
And in sharing our creations, we open ourselves up to the world,
And to the possibility of connection and understanding.

Through our art, we can express our deepest emotions,
And connect with others on a level that words cannot convey.
We can break down barriers, and bridge gaps in understanding,
And in doing so, we can create a more compassionate and harmonious world.

But let us also be mindful of the impact of our creations,
For they have the power to shape the world in both positive and negative ways.
Let us strive to create with purpose and intention,
And to use our talents for the betterment of all.

In conclusion, let us embrace the call of creativity,
But let us also remember our own humanity,
And strive to find balance between freedom and expression,
And to use our talents for the betterment of all.

Let our creativity be a force for good,
A way to connect, to understand and to move forward.
Let us be mindful of the impact of our creations,
And strive to create with purpose and intention.

And let us also remember that creativity is a journey,
A constant evolution and growth of the mind and the soul.
We must be willing to take risks, to experiment, and to make mistakes,
For it is through these experiences that we truly learn and grow.

We must not be afraid to push boundaries, to break conventions,
For it is through this that we can truly innovate and create something new.
But let us also be humble, and be open to criticism and feedback,
For it is through this that we can refine our work and improve.

And let us not forget that creativity is not just limited to the arts,
But it is a fundamental part of human existence.
It is the spark that drives us to explore, to invent, to discover,
And to create a better world for ourselves and future generations.

So let us embrace the call of creativity,
And let it guide us on our journey of self-discovery and expression.
Let us strive to find balance between freedom and art,
And to use our talents to make a positive impact on the world.

For it is through the pursuit of creativity,
That we can truly find purpose and fulfillment in life.

But let us also remember that the journey of creativity is not always easy,
It can be filled with doubts, struggles, and challenges,
It can be a lonely and isolating path,

And it can test our willpower, our patience and our determination.

It is important to remember that we are not alone in this journey,
That there are others who understand and share our struggles,
And that it is important to seek support and guidance from others,
Be it from friends, family, mentors or professionals.

We must also learn to take care of ourselves,
To nourish our bodies, minds and spirits,
For a healthy and balanced state of being,
Is a necessary foundation for any creative endeavor.

It is also important to remember that creativity is not just about the end product,
But also about the process, the journey, and the learning experience.
It is not about perfection or success,
But about the exploration, the experimentation and the growth.

So let us embrace the call of creativity,
And let it guide us on our journey of self-discovery and expression.
Let us strive to find balance between freedom and art,
And to use our talents to make a positive impact on the world.

But let us also remember that the journey of creativity is not always easy,
And that it is important to seek support, to take care of ourselves,
And to enjoy the process, the journey and the learning experience.

And let us not forget that creativity is not just something that is reserved for the
few,
But it is something that is innate in all of us.
We all have the potential to be creative,
To think outside the box, to see things differently, and to bring new ideas to the

table.

It is important to remember that creativity does not have to be limited to the
traditional arts,
But it can be applied to any field or area of life.
From science and technology, to business and politics,
Creativity can be a powerful tool for progress and advancement.

We must also remember that creativity is not just about the end result,
But about the journey of exploration, experimentation and learning.
It is about the process of problem-solving,
And the development of new ideas and ways of thinking.

So let us embrace the call of creativity,
And let it guide us on our journey of self-discovery and expression.
Let us strive to find balance between freedom and art,
And to use our talents to make a positive impact on the world.
But let us also remember that creativity is not just something that is reserved for
the few,
But it is something that is innate in all of us.
We all have the potential to be creative,
To think outside the box, to see things differently, and to bring new ideas to the
table.

And let us not be afraid to explore and experiment with our own creativity,
For it is through this that we can truly discover our own potential,
And make our own unique contributions to the world.

But let us also remember that creativity is not just about creating something new,
It is also about understanding, interpreting and appreciating the world around us.
It is about being open to different perspectives and ways of thinking,

And about being able to see beauty and value in the ordinary and mundane.

It is about being curious and inquisitive,
And about being willing to learn and grow.
It is about being able to see the world with fresh eyes,
And to be able to question and challenge the status quo.

And let us remember that creativity is not just about the final product,
But also about the journey and the process.
It is about the creativity that goes into the planning,
The experimentation, the learning, and the iteration.

In this way, we can recognize that creativity is not just a talent,
But a mindset, a way of thinking, and a way of living.
It is a constant exploration and discovery,
And it is something that can be nurtured and developed.

So let us embrace the call of creativity,
And let it guide us on our journey of self-discovery and expression.
Let us strive to find balance between freedom and art,
And to use our talents to make a positive impact on the world.
But let us also remember that creativity is not just something that is reserved for
the few,
It is something that is innate in all of us, and it is something that can be nurtured
and developed.

And let us not forget that creativity is not just about making something new,
But also about re-inventing and improving upon what already exists.
It is about being able to take something that already exists,
and to be able to see its potential and to push it to its limits.

It is about being able to see the potential in the world around us,
And to be able to use our talents and skills to make it better.
It is about being able to take something that is good,
And to make it great.

And let us also remember that creativity is not just
about making something new,
But also about making something that is meaningful,
That has a purpose, a message and a story to tell.
It is about being able to create something that is not just aesthetically pleasing,
But that is also emotionally resonant and impactful.

So let us embrace the call of creativity,
And let it guide us on our journey of self-discovery and expression.
Let us strive to find balance between freedom and art,
And to use our talents to make a positive impact on the world.
But let us also remember that creativity is not just something
that is reserved for the few,
It is something that is innate in all of us, and it is something
that can be nurtured and developed.
Let us use our creativity not just to create something new,
but also to improve upon what already exists,
And to create something that is meaningful, resonant and impactful.

15. In the Balance of Shadows: A Journey to Understanding

In deepest night, when all is still,
And moonlight dances on the hill,
A shadow creeps, a silent thrall,
A fleeting form upon the wall.

But what is this mysterious thing,
That follows us, yet never sings?
Is it a curse, a dark decree,
Or simply absence, void and free?

Science tells us of the light,
That travels far, in speed so bright,
But when it meets an obstacle,
A shadow forms, as if by ritual.

But shadows have a deeper tale,
A metaphor for life, a scale,
For all we are, and all we'll be,
Is but a shadow, cast by thee.

So let us not bemoan the dark,
For it is but a counterpart,
To all the light that guides our way,
And gives our shadows form and sway.

So let us dance with shadowed grace,
And in the light, find our own place,
For life and shadow are entwined,
And in the balance, we shall find.

But shadow is not just a thing of light,
It holds within it secrets quite.
It's not just absence, void and free,
But a reflection of one's own psyche.

Our inner demons and our fears,
Cast shadows on our lives, it appears,
And if we do not face them head on,
They'll consume us, till all is gone.

But if we dare to look within,
And face the shadows that begin,
We'll find a strength we didn't know,
And our shadows will begin to glow.

For in the darkness, there is power,
To heal and grow in any hour.
It is a teacher, full of grace,
Guiding us to a better place.

So let us not be afraid of shadow,
But embrace it, and let it go,
For in its depths, we'll find the light,
That guides us to the end of night.

For shadow is not just a thing of light,
It's a part of life, that holds insight,
It's not just absence, void and free,
But a reflection of one's own destiny.

But shadows also hold a deeper truth,
One that is often shrouded in youth.
For shadows are not just cast by light,
But by the actions of our own might.

Our deeds and choices, both good and bad,
Cast shadows that can make us glad,
Or fill our hearts with guilt and shame,
And leave us with a shadowed name.

But even in our darkest hour,
We have the power to empower,
To take control of our own fate,
And change the shadow we create.

For every action, there is a reaction,
And every choice, a chain of attraction,
We have the power to shape our fate,
And choose the shadow we wish to create.

So let us live with intention true,
And make our shadows bright and new,
For shadows are not just a thing of light,
But a reflection of our own might.

Let us embrace the shadows we cast,

And make them a thing of beauty at last,
For shadows are not just absence, void and free,
But a reflection of our own legacy.

Yet shadows are not just a product of our own making,
They also reflect the world in which we are partaking.
Society, culture, history, all cast their own shadows,
Shaping us, molding us, and sometimes, it shows.

We inherit the shadows of our forefathers and mothers,
The legacy of oppression, privilege, and others,
We must learn to recognize and acknowledge these shadows,
And actively work to dismantle the systems that hold them.

For only by understanding and facing these shadows,
Can we hope to bring about a brighter tomorrow.
It's a continuous process, that requires effort and care,
But through it, we can hope to create a world that is fair.

In conclusion, shadows are not just absence of light,
But a reflection of all that is, both dark and bright.
It's a reminder of the complexity and depth of existence,
And a call to action for growth, change, and persistence.

So let us not fear the shadows, but embrace them,
For they hold within them, the key to transcend.
Let us learn to dance in the moonlight,
With shadowed grace, towards a life that is right.

And as we journey through life, let us remember,
That shadows are not always dark, but can be a glimmer,

Of hope and beauty, if we choose to see them,
For they can be a source of inspiration and freedom.

In art, shadows add depth and dimension,
Creating a sense of realism and intention,
In literature, they add nuance and meaning,
Illuminating the human experience with a keenening.

Shadows can also be a source of mystery,
A canvas for the imagination and history,
They can be a playground for the mind and the soul,
A place to discover and explore, to make us whole.

Thus, shadows are not just a thing of the night,
But a part of life, that holds great insight,
It's not just absence, void and free,
But a reflection of the world and humanity.

So let us embrace the shadows in our lives,
And see them not as a hindrance, but as a guide,
For they can teach us about ourselves and the world,
And lead us to a deeper understanding and meaning.

Let us not be afraid to venture into the shadows,
For they can lead us to a greater understanding of our own morality,
And help us to make better choices and decisions,
That will lead to a more just and equitable society.

Shadows are not just a thing of darkness,
But a vital aspect of life, that holds great significance.
They are a reminder of the complexity and depth of existence,

And a call to action for growth, change, and persistence.

So let us embrace the shadows in our lives,
And see them not as a hindrance, but as a guide,
For they can lead us to a deeper understanding of ourselves and the world,
And help us to create a brighter and more just future for all.

And as we journey through life, let us not forget,
That shadows are not always negative, but can be a positive net.
They can bring balance and contrast,
And create a sense of harmony and art.

In nature, shadows are a part of the ecosystem,
Providing shelter and nourishment, a natural prism.
They can be a source of life and survival,
A reminder of the interconnectedness of all.

And in our own lives, shadows can be a source of growth,
A chance to learn and become more, to take an oath.
To become a better version of ourselves, to strive,
To bring about a change, to make a difference, to thrive.

So, let us not see shadows just as absence of light,
But as a necessary part of life, a natural insight.
Let us embrace them, learn from them and use them for good,
For in the balance of light and shadow lies a greater good.

And as we journey through life, let us also remember,
That shadows are not always something to overcome or surrender.
Sometimes, they can be a source of comfort and security,
A sanctuary from the harshness of reality.

In times of grief or loss, shadows can provide solace,
A place to heal and process, a way to cope and balance.
They can be a reminder of the ones we loved and lost,
And a way to keep them close, at any cost.

Shadows can also be a source of magic and wonder,
A place to dream and to ponder.
They can be a portal to the unknown,
A way to explore the mysteries of the world, alone.

Let us not see shadows as ominous and bleak,
But as a natural and necessary part of life, unique.
Let us embrace and appreciate the beauty and diversity,
Of the shadows that surround us, with humility and curiosity.

And as we continue on our journey, let us also acknowledge,
That shadows can be a source of fear and uncertainty,
But with courage and determination, we can learn to overcome,
And use our shadows as a tool for personal growth and self-becoming.

For shadows are not a curse, but a challenge,
An opportunity for self-discovery and self-empowerment,
A chance to learn and grow, to become stronger and braver,
And to rise above our fears, and become the best version of ourselves.

Let us not shy away from our shadows,
But embrace them and face them with a determined focus,
For in doing so, we can unlock our true potential,
And become the master of our own destiny, invincible.

Shadows are not just a thing of darkness,
But a vital aspect of life, that holds great significance.
They are a reminder of the complexity and depth of existence,
And a call to action for growth, change, and persistence.

And as we about to come to the end of this epic on shadow,
Let us reflect on all we have learned, and let it be so,
That we understand the power of shadows in our lives,
And how they shape us, guide us and help us to strive.

For shadows are not something to be feared or shunned,
But a natural and essential part of life that should be embraced and not shunned.
They can be a source of beauty, inspiration and growth,
And a means to unlock our true potential, that's worth the oath.

So let us continue to dance with shadowed grace,
And in the light, find our own pace,
For life and shadow are entwined,
And in the balance, we shall find,
A deeper understanding of ourselves and the world around,
And with that knowledge, our shadows shall no longer astound.

As we move forward, let us also remember,
That shadows are not always permanent, they can be temporary member.
Just as the sun rises and sets, creating shadows anew,
We too can change and evolve, our shadows can be outgrown too.

We have the power to change the direction of our light,
And thus change the shape of our shadows in the night,
We can work to improve ourselves and the world around,
And create new shadows that are brighter, more profound.

So let us not be held captive by our shadows,
Let us not let them define us, or make us cower,
For we have the power to change and grow,
And create a new shadow, that we can call our own.

Shadows are not just a thing of darkness,
But a vital aspect of life, that holds great significance.
They are a reminder of the complexity and depth of existence,
And a call to action for growth, change, and persistence.
Let us embrace our shadows, learn from them and use them for good,
For in the balance of light and shadow lies a greater good.

And as we continue on our journey, let us also be reminded,
That shadows are not always negative, they can be positive and kind.
They can bring balance and contrast,
And create a sense of harmony and art.

In fact, without shadows, there can be no light,
Without darkness, there can be no sight.
Without contrast, there can be of life, that holds great significance.
They are a reminder of the complexity and depth of existence,
And a call to action for growth, change, and persistence.
Let us embrace our shadows, learn from them and use them for good,
For in the balance of light and shadow lies a greater good.

Let us not fear the shadows, but see them as an opportunity,
a deeper understanding of ourselves and the world around us,
And let us use our shadows as a tool for personal growth and self-becoming.

Let us not shy away from the shadows, but face them head on,

And use their lessons to become stronger, more resilient and more wise.
Let us use our shadows as a guide to navigate the complexities of life,
And to create a brighter future for ourselves and for all mankind.

In conclusion, shadows are not just a thing of darkness,
But a vital aspect of life, that holds great significance.
They are a reminder of the complexity and depth of existence,
And a call to action for growth, change, and persistence.
Let us embrace our shadows, learn from them and use them for good,
For in the balance of light and shadow lies a greater good.
Let us walk with shadowed grace, towards a brighter tomorrow.

16. Pondering the Paradox of Pornography

In times of yore, man did oft ponder,
Upon the nature of the flesh, and how to squander
The carnal desires that did oft assail,
With visions of the flesh, both fair and frail.

But in this age of technology,
A new form of temptation doth one see,
Pornography, a scourge upon the mind,
A tool of Satan, of the devil designed.

With images and videos, so easily obtained,
The mind is flooded, and the soul is stained,
With images of lust, and carnal desire,
The will is weakened, and the moral fire.

But is this vice truly a sin,
Or simply a natural inclination within?
Is the human desire for sexual pleasure,
A base instinct, that we should treasure?

The philosophers of old did oft debate,
The nature of desire, and its innate,
Place in the human experience,
Some decried it, while others did fence.

But in this modern age, we can see,
The effects of pornography, so easily,
The addiction, the objectification, the harm,
All evidence of its negative charm.

And yet, still the question doth remain,
Is it a vice, or a natural gain?
Perhaps the answer is not so clear,
But one thing is certain, it doth not bring cheer.

So let us ponder, and let us weigh,
The effects of pornography, both night and day,
And strive for a balance, between our desire,
And the well-being of our entire.

As we delve deeper into this quandary,
We must also consider society's mentality,
For pornography, in its abundance,
Has led to a distorted view of love and courtship.

Gone are the days of courtship and romance,
Replaced by a shallow and fleeting chance,
To satisfy our base desires and needs,
Without any thought of the other's wants and needs.

But as with all things in life, moderation is key,
In our consumption of pornography, we must be wary,
For too much indulgence can lead to harm,
But a healthy dose, need not raise alarm.

As we navigate this complex issue,
We must remember, it's not just about the individual's,
But also the collective impact on society,
And how we can create a healthier, more balanced community.

So let us not be quick to judge,
But rather, let us strive to understand,
The nature of this controversial topic,
And work towards a solution that is just and authentic.

For in the end, it is not just about the act,
But about the way it shapes our thought and our tact,
As we strive for a better understanding,
Of the human experience, and the nature of human demanding.

As we delve deeper still, into the depths of this discourse,
We must also consider the impact on the individual's remorse,
For those who become addicted to pornography,
Suffering can be severe, both mentally and emotionally.

With constant access to endless streams of content,
Addiction can develop, in ways that are bent,
On consuming more and more, in a never-ending quest,
To satisfy the desires that lay within our breast.

But as with any addiction, there is hope,
For those who seek help, and learn to cope,
With the underlying issues that drive their addiction,
Recovery is possible, with the right intervention.

But it's not just about the individual,

The societal impact must also be considered,
For as we continue to consume and produce,
Pornography at an alarming rate,

We must also think about how it shapes our views,
On relationships, sex and consent,
And work towards creating a culture,
Where healthy attitudes towards sex are the norm.

Pornography is a complex issue,
That requires a multifaceted approach to address,
Let us strive for balance, and a better understanding,
As we navigate the complexities of human demanding.

And as we move forward, let us not forget,
The importance of consent, and the respect,
That all individuals deserve,
In their sexual experiences, they must be heard.

For pornography, when consumed with care,
Can be a tool for education and exploration,
But when consumed in excess, it can be a snare,
Leading to objectification and exploitation.

As a society, we must strive to create,
A culture where consent is not just a debate,
But a fundamental principle, upheld with pride,
In all aspects of sexual interactions, worldwide.

And so, as we ponder on this topic,
Let us not forget, the importance of consent and the proper ethic,

For only then, can we truly create a culture,
Where the consumption of pornography is not a vulture.

In the end, it is up to us, as individuals,
To take responsibility for our own sexual behaviors,
And to work towards creating a society,
Where the consumption of pornography is done with maturity and sobriety.

But as we move forward, let us not be blind,
To the fact that, for some, pornography is not just a matter of mind,
For some are forced into the industry, against their will,
Victims of human trafficking, a story of terror and thrill.

The dark side of the industry must not be ignored,
For the exploitation and abuse must be abhorred,
We must take a stand against such injustice,
And work towards creating a world where exploitation is not a part of our
existence.

And so, as we ponder this topic,
Let us not forget, the importance of consent and the proper ethic,
But also the need to address the darker side of the industry,
And work towards creating a society,
where all individuals are treated with dignity and dignity.

In the end, it is up to us, as individuals,
To take responsibility for our own actions and behaviors,
And to work towards creating a society,
Where the consumption of pornography
is done with awareness and empathy.

As we conclude our epic on pornography,
Let us not forget the role of education,
In shaping our understanding,
Of this complex and nuanced topic of human desire.

For the only way to truly address,
The issues surrounding pornography,
Is through open and honest discussion,
And the dissemination of accurate information.

Education on healthy relationships,
Consent, and the harms of addiction,
Can empower individuals to make informed choices,
And to navigate the complexities of human desire with discretion.

But education alone is not enough,
We must also work towards creating,
A society that values consent and respect,
And where the exploitation and abuse of individuals is not tolerated.

It is a challenging task, but one that must be undertaken,
As we strive to create a culture,
Where the consumption of pornography is done with responsibility and care,
And the well-being of all individuals is at the forefront, everywhere.

And as we move forward, it is essential,
To remember that the issue of pornography,
Is not just a personal one,
But one that is deeply intertwined with our culture, our society and our economy.

For the porn industry is a multi-billion dollar enterprise,

That touches many aspects of our lives,
From the way we consume media,
To the way we think about sex, relationships and gender.

Therefore, any attempts to address this issue,
Must be holistic in nature,
And take into account, the various forces at play,
That contribute to the perpetuation of the problem.

As we come to the end of our epic,
It is important to remember,
That the issue of pornography is not a simple one,
But a complex and multifaceted topic that requires
nuanced discussion and continuous exploration.

As we reflect on the subject of pornography,
We must also consider the impact it has on the younger generation,
For with the easy accessibility of the internet,
Children and teenagers are exposed to it at a younger age than ever before.

The effects of early exposure to pornography,
Can be damaging to their developing minds,
Distorting their understanding of healthy relationships,
And leading to a host of emotional and psychological issues.

Therefore, it is crucial, that we as a society,
Take steps to protect our young,
Through education, parental control and age-restriction,
To ensure that they are not exposed to it before
they are emotionally and mentally ready to process it.

We must also address the issue of consent,
In the context of children and teenagers,
Ensuring that they understand the importance of consent,
And that they are not exposed to content
that is violent, non-consensual or exploitative.

17. Marriage in the Modern Age: A Reflection on the Sacred Bond

In ancient times, when man and woman didst join in matrimony,

A sacred bond was formed, a union divine,

A blending of two souls, a perfect harmony,

A love that would endure through all eternity.

But alas, in these modern times, the sanctity of marriage

Is oft called into question, its very essence marred.

Marriage, a sacred rite, a binding of two hearts,

A pact of love and loyalty, a solemn vow,

A promise to stand together through all life's starts,

A commitment to cherish and to nurture now.

But in these times of change, the institution is marred,

As men and women seek to redefine matrimony.

Matrimony, a sacred bond, a sacred tie,

A union of two souls, a love eternal,

A covenant to stand together, side by side,

Through all the joys and sorrows, good and evil,

But in this age of reason, the sacred is marred,

As men and women seek to sever the marriage vow.

Vow, a promise made, a sacred oath,

A pledge to love and cherish, to honor and obey,

A commitment to stand together, through all life's growth,

A bond that should last until death doth us part.

But in these times of change, the vow is marred,

As men and women seek to redefine matrimony.

Matrimony, a sacred bond, a sacred trust,
A union of two souls, a love unchanging,
A covenant to stand together, to always be just,
To love and to cherish, through all life's ranging.
But in this age of progress, the sacred is marred,
As men and women seek to break the marriage vow.
Vow, a promise made, a sacred promise,
A pledge to love and cherish, to honor and obey,
A commitment to stand together, through all life's chaos,
A bond that should last until death doth us part.
But in these times of change, the vow is marred,
As men and women seek to redefine matrimony.
Matrimony, a sacred bond, a sacred union,
A blending of two souls, a perfect harmony,
A love that should endure through all eternity,
But in this age of reason, the sacred is marred,
As men and women seek to break the marriage vow.
Vow, a promise made, a sacred pledge,
But in these times of change, the vow is marred,
As men and women seek to redefine matrimony.
A sacred bond, a union divine,
But alas, in these modern times, the sanctity of marriage
Is oft called into question, its very essence marred.
And so, in this age of confusion,
The sacred bond of matrimony is oft besmirched,
As men and women seek to redefine their union,
To suit their own desires and whims, perchance.
But in doing so, they forget the true purpose,
Of marriage, a sacred bond, a sacred trust.
Trust, a cornerstone of any union,
A foundation upon which love doth flourish,

But in this age of self-centeredness, trust is marred,
As men and women seek to put themselves first,
Forgetting the sacred bond of matrimony,
And the promise of a love eternal, made in vow.
Vow, a sacred pledge, a promise made,
A commitment to love and cherish, to honor and obey,
But in this age of individualism, vows are marred,
As men and women seek to put their own wants first,
Forgetting the sacred bond of matrimony,
And the trust that lies at the heart of any union.
Union, a sacred bond, a blending of two souls,
A perfect harmony, a love unchanging,
But in this age of fleeting passions, unions are marred,
As men and women seek to seek pleasure first,
Forgetting the sacred bond of matrimony,
And the vow to love and cherish, made with trust.
Trust, a cornerstone of any union,
A foundation upon which love doth flourish,
But in this age of fleeting fancies, trust is marred,
As men and women seek to put their own desires first,
Forgetting the sacred bond of matrimony,
And the vow to love and cherish, made in sacred trust.
Trust, a sacred bond, a sacred promise,
A pledge to love and cherish, to honor and obey,
But in this age of self-indulgence, trust is marred,
As men and women seek to put themselves first,
Forgetting the sacred bond of matrimony,
And the union that should endure through all eternity.
Eternity, a promise of love that should endure,
A bond that should last until death doth us part,
But in this age of fleeting fancies, eternity is marred,

As men and women seek to put their own wants first,
Forgetting the sacred bond of matrimony,
And the vow to love and cherish, made with trust.
Trust, a cornerstone of any union,
A foundation upon which love doth flourish,
But in this age of self-centeredness, trust is marred,
As men and women seek to put themselves first,
Forgetting the sacred bond of matrimony,
And the eternity that true love doth promise.
Promise, a sacred pledge, a sacred vow,
A commitment to love and cherish, to honor and obey,
But in this age of fleeting passions, promises are marred,
As men and women seek to put their own wants first,
Forgetting the sacred bond of matrimony,
And the trust that lies at the heart of any union.
Union, a sacred bond, a blending of two souls,
A perfect harmony, a love unchanging,
But in this age of self-indulgence, unions are marred,
As men and women seek to put themselves first,
Forgetting the sacred bond of matrimony,
And the promise of a love eternal, made in vow.
Vow, a sacred pledge, a promise made,
A commitment to love and cherish, to honor and obey,
But in this age of fleeting fancies, vows are marred,
As men and women seek to put their own wants first,
Forgetting the sacred bond of matrimony,
And the trust that lies at the heart of any union.
Union, a sacred bond, a blending of two souls,
A perfect harmony, a love unchanging,
But in this age of self-indulgence, unions are marred,
As men and women seek to put themselves first,

Forgetting the sacred bond of matrimony,
And the vow to love and cherish, made with trust.
Trust, a cornerstone of any union,
A foundation upon which love doth flourish,
But in this age of fleeting passions, trust is marred,
As men and women seek to seek pleasure first,
Forgetting the sacred bond of matrimony,
And the union that should endure through all eternity.
Eternity, a promise of love that should endure,
A bond that should last until death doth us part,
But in this age of self-centeredness, eternity is marred,
As men and women seek to put their own desires first,
Forgetting the sacred bond of matrimony,
And the vow to love and cherish, made with trust.
Trust, a sacred bond, a sacred promise,
A pledge to love and cherish, to honor and obey,
But in this age of fleeting fancies, trust is marred,
As men and women seek to put their own wants first,
Forgetting the sacred bond of matrimony,
And the union that should endure through all eternity.
Eternity, a promise of love that should endure,
A bond that should last until death doth us part,
But in this age of self-indulgence, eternity is marred,
As men and women seek to put themselves first,
Forgetting the sacred bond of matrimony,
And the trust that lies at the heart of any union.
Union, a sacred bond, a blending of two souls,
A perfect harmony, a love unchanging,
But in this age of confusion, unions are marred,
As men and women seek to redefine their union,
Forgetting the sacred bond of matrimony,

And the promise of a love eternal, made in vow.
Vow, a sacred pledge, a promise made,
A commitment to love and cherish, to honor and obey,
But in this age of self-centeredness, vows are marred,
As men and women seek to put themselves first,
Forgetting the sacred bond of matrimony,
And the trust that lies at the heart of any union.
Union, a sacred bond, a blending of two souls,
A perfect harmony, a love unchanging,
But in this age of fleeting passions, unions are marred,
As men and women seek to seek pleasure first,
Forgetting the sacred bond of matrimony,
And the eternity that true love doth promise.
Promise, a sacred pledge, a sacred vow,
A commitment to love and cherish, to honor and obey,
But in this age of self-indulgence, promises are marred,
As men and women seek to put themselves first,
Forgetting the sacred bond of matrimony,
And the trust that lies at the heart of any union.
Union, a sacred bond, a blending of two souls,
A perfect harmony, a love unchanging,
But in this age of confusion, unions are marred,
As men and women
seek to redefine their union,
Forgetting the sacred bond of matrimony,
And the promise of a love eternal, made in vow.
Vow, a sacred pledge, a promise made,
A commitment to love and cherish, to honor and obey,
But in this age of fleeting fancies, vows are marred,
As men and women seek to put their own wants first,
Forgetting the sacred bond of matrimony,

And the union that should endure through all eternity.
Eternity, a promise of love that should endure,
A bond that should last until death doth us part,
But in this age of self-centeredness, eternity is marred,
As men and women seek to put themselves first,
Forgetting the sacred bond of matrimony,
And the trust that lies at the heart of any union.
Union, a sacred bond, a blending of two souls,
A perfect harmony, a love unchanging,
But in this age of confusion, unions are marred,
As men and women seek to redefine their union,
Forgetting the sacred bond of matrimony,
And the promise of a love eternal, made in vow.
Vow, a sacred pledge, a promise made,
A commitment to love and cherish, to honor and obey,
But in this age of fleeting passions, vows are marred,
As men and women seek to seek pleasure first,
Forgetting the sacred bond of matrimony,
And the trust that lies at the heart of any union.
Union, a sacred bond, a blending of two souls,
A perfect harmony, a love unchanging,
But in this age of self-indulgence, unions are marred,
As men and women seek to put themselves first,
Forgetting the sacred bond of matrimony,
And the eternity that true love doth promise.
Promise, a sacred pledge, a sacred vow,
A commitment to love and cherish, to honor and obey,
But in this age of fleeting fancies, promises are marred,
As men and women seek to put their own wants first,
Forgetting the sacred bond of matrimony,
And the union that should endure through all eternity.

Eternity, a promise of love that should endure,
A bond that should last until death doth us part,
But in this age of self-centeredness, eternity is marred,
As men and women seek to put themselves first,
Forgetting the sacred bond of matrimony,
And the trust that lies at the heart of any union.
Union, a sacred bond, a blending of two souls,
A perfect harmony, a love unchanging,
But in this age of confusion, unions are marred,
As men and women seek to redefine their union,
Forgetting the sacred bond of matrimony,
And the vow to love and cherish, made with trust.
Trust, a cornerstone of any union,
A foundation upon which love doth flourish,
But in this age of fleeting fancies, trust is marred,
As men and women seek to put their own wants first,
Forgetting the sacred bond of matrimony,
And the promise of a love eternal, made in vow.
Vow, a sacred pledge, a promise made,
A commitment to love and cherish, to honor and obey,
But in this age of self-indulgence, vows are marred,
As men and women seek to put themselves first,
Forgetting the sacred bond of matrimony
And the trust that lies at the heart of any union.
Union, a sacred bond, a blending of two souls,
A perfect harmony, a love unchanging,
But in this age of fleeting fancies, unions are marred,
As men and women seek to put their own wants first,
Forgetting the sacred bond of matrimony,
And the vow to love and cherish, made with trust.
Trust, a cornerstone of any union,

A foundation upon which love doth flourish,
But in this age of self-centeredness, trust is marred,
As men and women seek to put themselves first,
Forgetting the sacred bond of matrimony,
And the promise of a love eternal, made in vow.
Vow, a sacred pledge, a promise made,
A commitment to love and cherish, to honor and obey,
But in this age of fleeting passions, vows are marred,
As men and women seek to seek pleasure first,
Forgetting the sacred bond of matrimony,
And the trust that lies at the heart of any union.
Union, a sacred bond, a blending of two souls,
A perfect harmony, a love unchanging,
But in this age of confusion, unions are marred,
As men and women seek to redefine their union,
Forgetting the sacred bond of matrimony,
And the vow to love and cherish, made with trust.
Trust, a cornerstone of any union,
A foundation upon which love doth flourish,
But in this age of self-indulgence, trust is marred,
As men and women seek to put themselves first,
Forgetting the sacred bond of matrimony,
And the promise of a love eternal, made in vow.
Vow, a sacred pledge, a promise made,
A commitment to love and cherish, to honor and obey,
But in this age of fleeting fancies, vows are marred,
As men and women seek to put their own wants first,
Forgetting the sacred bond of matrimony,
And the union that should endure through all eternity.
Eternity, a promise of love that should endure,
A bond that should last until death doth us part,

But in this age of self-centeredness, eternity is marred,
As men and women seek to put themselves first,
Forgetting the sacred bond of matrimony,
And the trust that lies at the heart of any union.
Union, a sacred bond, a blending of two souls,
A perfect harmony, a love unchanging,
But in this age of confusion, unions are marred,
As men and women seek to redefine their union,
Forgetting the sacred bond of matrimony,
And the vow to love and cherish, made with trust.
Trust, a cornerstone of any union,
A foundation upon which love doth flourish,
But in this age of self-indulgence, trust is marred,
As men and women seek to put themselves first,
Forgetting the sacred bond of matrimony,
And the promise of a love eternal, made in vow.
Vow, a sacred pledge, a promise made,
A commitment to love and cherish, to honor and obey,
But in this age of fleeting fancies, vows are marred,
As men and women seek to put their own wants first,
Forgetting the sacred bond of matrimony,
And the trust that lies at the heart of any union.
Union, a sacred bond, a blending of two souls,
A perfect harmony, a love unchanging,
But in this age of fleeting fancies, unions are marred,
As men and women seek to put their own wants first,
Forgetting the sacred bond of matrimony,
And the vow to love and cherish, made with trust.
Trust, a cornerstone of any union,
A foundation upon which love doth flourish,
But in this age of self-centeredness, trust is marred,

As men and women seek to put themselves first,
Forgetting the sacred bond of matrimony,
And the promise of a love eternal, made in vow.
Vow, a sacred pledge, a promise made,
A commitment to love and cherish, to honor and obey,
But in this age of fleeting passions, vows are marred,
As men and women seek to seek pleasure first,
Forgetting the sacred bond of matrimony,
And the trust that lies at the heart of any union.
Union, a sacred bond, a blending of two souls,
A perfect harmony, a love unchanging,
But in this age of confusion, unions are marred,
As men and women seek to redefine their union,
Forgetting the sacred bond of matrimony,
And the vow to love and cherish, made with trust.
Trust, a cornerstone of any union,
A foundation upon which love doth flourish,
But in this age of self-indulgence, trust is marred,
As men and women seek to put themselves first,
Forgetting the sacred bond of matrimony,
And the promise of a love eternal, made in vow.
Vow, a sacred pledge, a promise made,
A commitment to love and cherish, to honor and obey,
But in this age of fleeting fancies, vows are marred,
As men and women seek to put their own wants first,
Forgetting the sacred bond of matrimony,
And the trust that lies at the heart of any union.
Union, a sacred bond, a blending of two souls,
A perfect harmony, a love unchanging,
But in this age of confusion, unions are marred,
As men and women seek to redefine their union,

Forgetting the sacred bond of matrimony,
And the vow to love and cherish, made with trust.
Trust, a cornerstone of any union,
A foundation upon which love doth flourish,
But in this age of self-indulgence, trust is marred,
As men and women seek to put themselves first,
Forgetting the sacred bond of matrimony,
And the promise of a love eternal, made in vow.
Vow, a sacred pledge, a promise made,
A commitment to love and cherish, to honor and obey,
But in this age of fleeting fancies, vows are marred,
As men and women seek to put their own wants first,
Forgetting the sacred bond of matrimony,
And the union that should endure through all eternity.
Eternity, a promise of love that should endure,
A bond that should last until death doth us part,
But in this age of self-centeredness, eternity is marred,
As men and women seek to put themselves first,
Forgetting the sacred bond of matrimony,
And the trust that lies at the heart of any union.
Union, a sacred bond, a blending of two souls,
A perfect harmony, a love unchanging,
But in this age of confusion,
unions are marred,
As men and women seek to redefine their union,
Forgetting the sacred bond of matrimony,
And the vow to love and cherish, made with trust.
Trust, a cornerstone of any union,
A foundation upon which love doth flourish,
But in this age of self-indulgence, trust is marred,
As men and women seek to put themselves first,

Forgetting the sacred bond of matrimony,
And the promise of a love eternal, made in vow.
Vow, a sacred pledge, a promise made,
A commitment to love and cherish, to honor and obey,
But in this age of fleeting fancies, vows are marred,
As men and women seek to put their own wants first,
Forgetting the sacred bond of matrimony,
And the trust that lies at the heart of any union.
Union, a sacred bond, a blending of two souls,
A perfect harmony, a love unchanging,
But in this age of confusion, unions are marred,
As men and women seek to redefine their union,
Forgetting the sacred bond of matrimony,
And the vow to love and cherish, made with trust.
Trust, a cornerstone of any union,
A foundation upon which love doth flourish,
But in this age of self-indulgence, trust is marred,
As men and women seek to put themselves first,
Forgetting the sacred bond of matrimony,
And the promise of a love eternal, made in vow.
Vow, a sacred pledge, a promise made,
A commitment to love and cherish, to honor and obey,
But in this age of fleeting fancies, vows are marred,
As men and women seek to put their own wants first,
Forgetting the sacred bond of matrimony,
And the trust that lies at the heart of any union.
Union, a sacred bond, a blending of two souls,
A perfect harmony, a love unchanging,
But in this age of confusion, unions are marred,
As men and women seek to redefine their union,
Forgetting the sacred bond of matrimony,

And the vow to love and cherish, made with trust.
Trust, a cornerstone of any union,
A foundation upon which love doth flourish,
But in this age of self-indulgence, trust is marred,
As men and women seek to put themselves first,
Forgetting the sacred bond of matrimony,
And the promise of a love eternal, made in vow.
Vow, a sacred pledge, a promise made,
A commitment to love and cherish, to honor and obey,
But in this age of fleeting fancies, vows are marred,
As men and women seek to put their own wants first,
Forgetting the sacred bond of matrimony,
And the trust that lies at the heart of any union.
Union, a sacred bond, a blending of two souls,
A perfect harmony, a love unchanging,
But in this age of confusion, unions are marred,
As men and women seek to redefine their union,
Forgetting the sacred bond of matrimony,
And the vow to love and cherish, made with trust.
Trust, a cornerstone of any union,
A foundation upon which love doth flourish,
But in this age of self-indulgence, trust is marred,
As men and women seek to put themselves first,
Forgetting the sacred bond of matrimony
And the promise of a love eternal, made in vow.

Vow, a sacred pledge, a promise made,
A commitment to love and cherish, to honor and obey,
But in this age of fleeting fancies, vows are marred,
As men and women seek to put their own wants first,
Forgetting the sacred bond of matrimony,

And the trust that lies at the heart of any union.

Union, a sacred bond, a blending of two souls,
A perfect harmony, a love unchanging,
But in this age of confusion, unions are marred,
As men and women seek to redefine their union,
Forgetting the sacred bond of matrimony,
And the vow to love and cherish, made with trust.

Trust, a cornerstone of any union,
A foundation upon which love doth flourish,
But in this age of self-indulgence, trust is marred,
As men and women seek to put themselves first,
Forgetting the sacred bond of matrimony,
And the promise of a love eternal, made in vow.

Vow, a sacred pledge, a promise made,
A commitment to love and cherish, to honor and obey,
But in this age of fleeting fancies, vows are marred,
As men and women seek to put their own wants first,
Forgetting the sacred bond of matrimony,
And the trust that lies at the heart of any union.

Union, a sacred bond, a blending of two souls,
A perfect harmony, a love unchanging,
But in this age of confusion, unions are marred,
As men and women seek to redefine their union,
Forgetting the sacred bond of matrimony,
And the vow to love and cherish, made with trust.

Trust, a cornerstone of any union,

A foundation upon which love doth flourish,
But in this age of self-indulgence, trust is marred,
As men and women seek to put themselves first,
Forgetting the sacred bond of matrimony,
And the promise of a love eternal, made in vow.

Vow, a sacred pledge, a promise made,
A commitment to love and cherish, to honor and obey,
But in this age of fleeting fancies, vows are marred,
As men and women seek to put their own wants first,
Forgetting the sacred bond of matrimony,
And the trust that lies at the heart of any union.

Union, a sacred bond, a blending of two souls,
A perfect harmony, a love unchanging,
But in this age of confusion, unions are marred,
As men and women seek to redefine their union,
Forgetting the sacred bond of matrimony,
And the vow to love and cherish, made with trust.

But let us not despair, for there are those who still abide,
By the sacred bond of matrimony,
And the vow to love and cherish, made with trust,
For these unions, though marred by time,
Shall forever flourish, in perfect harmony,
As a shining example for all to obey.

Obey, the call of love and honor,
To put others before ourselves,
For in doing so, we shall find true union,
A sacred bond, a blending of two souls,

A perfect harmony, a love unchanging,
And the vow to love and cherish, made with trust.

Trust, the foundation of any union,
A sacred pledge, a promise made,

A commitment to love and cherish, to honor and obey,
But in this age of fleeting fancies, trust is marred,
As men and women seek to put their own wants first,
Forgetting the sacred bond of matrimony,
And the vow to love and cherish, made with trust.

Trust, the foundation of any union,
A sacred pledge, a promise made,
A commitment to love and cherish, to honor and obey,
But in this age of fleeting fancies, trust is marred,
As men and women seek to put their own wants first,
Forgetting the sacred bond of matrimony,
And the vow to love and cherish, made with trust.

Trust, the foundation of any union,
A sacred pledge, a promise made,
A commitment to love and cherish, to honor and obey,
But in this age of fleeting fancies, trust is marred,
As men and women seek to put their own wants first,
Forgetting the sacred bond of matrimony,
And the vow to love and cherish, made with trust.

Trust, the foundation of any union,
A sacred pledge, a promise made,
A commitment to love and cherish, to honor and obey,

But in this age of fleeting fancies, trust is marred,
As men and women seek to put their own wants first,
Forgetting the sacred bond of matrimony,
And the vow to love and cherish, made with trust.

Trust, the foundation of any union,
A sacred pledge, a promise made,
A commitment to love and cherish, to honor and obey,
But in this age of fleeting fancies, trust is marred,
As men and women seek to put their own wants first,
Forgetting the sacred bond of matrimony,
And the vow to love and cherish, made with trust.

Trust, the foundation of any union,
A sacred pledge, a promise made,
A commitment to love and cherish, to honor and obey,
But in this age of fleeting fancies, trust is marred,
As men and women seek to put their own wants first,
Forgetting the sacred bond of matrimony,
And the vow to love and cherish, made with trust.

Trust, the foundation of any union,
A sacred pledge, a promise made,
A commitment to love and cherish, to honor and obey,
But in this age of fleeting fancies, trust is marred,
As men and women seek to put their own wants first,
Forgetting the sacred bond of matrimony,
And the vow to love and cherish, made with trust.

But let us not despair, for there are those who still abide,
By the sacred bond of matrimony,

And the vow to love and cherish, made with trust,
For these unions, though marred by time,
Shall forever flourish, in perfect harmony,
As a shining example for all to obey.

Obey, the call of love and honor,
To put others before ourselves,
For in doing so, we shall find true union,
A sacred bond, a blending of two souls,
A perfect harmony, a love unchanging,
And the vow to love and cherish, made with trust.

Trust, the foundation of any union,
A sacred pledge, a promise made,
A commitment to love and cherish, to honor and obey,
But in this age of fleeting fancies, trust is marred,
As men and women seek to put their own wants first,
Forgetting the sacred bond of matrimony,
And the vow to love and cherish, made with trust.

But let us not forget the science of love,
For it is not just a feeling, but a chemical reaction,
A dance between hormones and neurotransmitters,
That creates the bond of matrimony,
And the vow to love and cherish, made with trust.

But let us not forget the philosophy of love,
For it is not just a feeling, but a decision,
A choice to commit to another,
To honor and obey, to love and cherish,
And the vow to love and cherish, made with trust.

But let us not forget the cryptic nature of love,
For it is not always easy to understand,
It is a mystery, a puzzle, a code to decipher,
But when unlocked, it creates the bond of matrimony,
And the vow to love and cherish, made with trust.

For in the end, love is all these things,
Science, philosophy, and cryptic mystery,
But it is also a commitment, a vow,
To love and cherish, to honor and obey,
A sacred bond, the foundation of matrimony,
And the vow to love and cherish, made with trust.

Trust, the foundation of any union,
A sacred pledge, a promise made,
A commitment to love and cherish, to honor and obey,
But in this age of fleeting fancies, trust is marred,
As men and women seek to put their own wants first,
Forgetting the sacred bond of matrimony,
And the vow to love and cherish, made with trust.

But let us not forget, that true love endures,
For in the face of all obstacles, it stands strong,
And the bond of matrimony, and the vow to love and cherish,
Made with trust, shall forever be a shining example,
For all to honor, obey, and strive for in their own unions.

Khublei Shihajar Nguh

"A Sonnet for Our Dear Readers"
Oh readers, we do thank you from our hearts,
For taking time to delve into our book,
And for the journey that you've taken, starts
And ends within its pages, take a look!
We promise, as a reward for your time,
A cup of coffee, when we meet one day,
And bring the book, so we can share the climb,
And chat about its contents, in a way!
For laughter, wit, and humor, we'll impart,
And share a smile, a joke, a silly rhyme,
And raise a cup, in celebration, start,
Of knowledge, gained, and memories, divine.
So here's to you, our dear and cherished readers,
For making our work, a joy, a true treasurers.
And may this book, be a source of delight,
That brings you joy, both day and night.
And when we meet, we'll raise a toast,
To friendship, laughter, and this book we boast.
So let us gather, with a cup in hand,
And share a laugh, and stories, oh so grand.
And let us cherish, this moment in time,
As we celebrate, our love for the written rhyme.
So here's to you, our dear and cherished readers,
For making our work, a joy, a true treasurers.

Note

As I, a breviloquent raptor, wield A lever, with naught else to my design, I generate tones for the aural field In this prosaic orb we call mankind. My actions, though, are but a small part Of forces far beyond my control, For nature holds the key to each chart And sets the laws that govern the whole. But still, I am compelled to explore The workings of this vast machinery, To seek the truth that lies at core And find the answers to humanity. Though some may call it quest I'll seek the truth, with no time to rest.

About The Author

Meet Mawphniang, a man of many parts,
A lawyer, entrepreneur, and more,
With boundless curiosity, and open heart,
And a passion for life, that he will explore.
With talent, drive, and a thirst for success,
He has achieved much, in the professional sphere,
But it is in writing, where he finds the best,
And where his true passion, shines so clear.
With boundless curiosity and verve,
He embraces new ideas, with an open mind,
And ventures boldly, into unknown lands,
With fearlessness, that is truly one of a kind.
From Syadheh Village, in Ri Bhoi District,
He hails, a soul ever-striving, never at rest.
And as he writes his story, with fearlessness,
He makes the most of every moment, ever-unfurled.
And though his journey, may take many roads,
Each step, a step toward self-discovery,
With every word, he shares his soul's abode,
And invites us all, to join in, and be.
For Mawphniang, life is a precious gift,
To be cherished, and explored, with all one's might,
And as he writes, he lifts, our spirits, and uplifts,
With tales of wonder, and delight.
So let us follow, this soul ever-striving,
And be inspired, by his boundless energy,
For Mawphniang, is a man truly thriving,
In a world, that he makes, all the more lovely.

And as we read, his words, so full of life,
We too, shall be, forever, changed by his strife.
And though his journey, may be filled with strife,
He never loses sight, of what is true,
For he knows, that in the end, it is life,
That gives us meaning, and a purpose too.
And so, he writes, with a heart full of love,
And a mind, that is always seeking more,
For he knows, that in the depths, of the dove,
Lies the answers, to life's great riddle, and score.
And as we read, his words, so full of grace,
We too, shall be, forever, touched by his pen,
For Mawphniang, is a man, with a gentle face,
And a heart, that is always, filled with love again.
So let us cherish, this soul ever-striving,
And be inspired, by his boundless energy.

By A - Team

P.C : Clarissa Candace Giri